"Gordon Stewart has a way with words, a clean, clear, concise, and yet still creative way with words, a way that can set the reader almost simultaneously at the blood-stained center of the timely—the urgent issues of our day—and also at the deep heart of the timeless, those eternal questions that have forever challenged the human mind. Stewart looks at terror, Isis, and all their kin, from the perspective of Paul Tillich and, yes, John Lennon. He moves from Paris, Maine, by way of the town drunk, toward the City of God. This is strong medicine, to be taken in small, but serious doses. Wear a crash helmet!"

—J. Barrie Shepherd

Author of *Between Mirage and Miracle*

"*Be Still!* is needed at this American moment of collective madness even more than the moments that occasioned many of the essays originally airing on public radio and other venues. With a keen eye and a knack for telling the right story at the right time, Rev. Stewart speaks to the pressing issues in our politics, economy, and culture, and consistently, often poignantly, puts them in ethical and theological perspective that clarifies what too often mystifies. Great bedside reading for those of us who stay up at night concerned about where our world is heading!"

—Michael McNally, Ph.D

Professor of Religion, Carleton College; Author of *Honoring Elders*

"*Be Still!: Departure from Collective Madness*, is exactly what its title proclaims: a departure from the frenzy and folly of our times. Each essay offers the reader an opportunity to breathe deep, to fall into the story or idea and consider what it means to be a citizen, a friend, a human being. The topics covered are both particular and universal (usually both at the same time), and the writing is wonderfully concise and open—much like poetry! This is a book you will want to open again and again; it's what the world needs now, more than ever."

—Joyce Sutphen

Minnesota Poet Laureate; Professor in English, Gustavus Adolphus College

"In *Be Still!* Stewart masterfully spins a counter-narrative to the collective madness that is gripping our world. Like the psalmist, Stewart prays thoughtfully through metaphors and religious tradition, meshing theologians with news headlines to lead the reader to a deeper, more sustained truth. *Be Still!* reads like part op-ed and part parable. In these troubling and anxious times, may we, who have ears to hear, listen!"

—Frank M. Yamada

President, McCormick Theological Seminary

Be Still!

BE STILL!

Departure from Collective Madness

Gordon C. Stewart

Foreword by Eric Ringham

Introduction by Wayne G. Boulton

WIPF & STOCK · Eugene, Oregon

BE STILL!
Departure from Collective Madness

Wipf & Stock
An Imprint of Wipf and Stock Publishers
199 W. 8th Ave., Suite 3
Eugene, OR 97401

www.wipfandstock.com

PAPERBACK ISBN: 978-1-4982-8292-5
HARDCOVER ISBN: 978-1-4982-8294-9
EBOOK ISBN: 978-1-4982-8293-2

Manufactured in the USA. 01/04/17

Thanks to MinnPost.com for copyright permission for use of previously published commentaries:

"Reframing the gun conversation," October 22, 2015.
"Homeland militarization—tanks in Ferguson, Blackhawks in Minneapolis — must be stopped," August 22, 2014.
"They may squirm in hearings, but Wall Street oligarchs know who has the power," April 29, 2010.
"Gulf oil-spill crisis raises basic questions about how we think of ourselves," June 4, 2010.
"For faith and for politics, there is one over-riding question: Am I my brother's keeper?" January 6, 2010.
"How appeals to fear—and misuse of Scripture—dampened a chilidog celebration," October 9, 2009.
"Blackwater/Xe: How did it happen that the US came to rely on mercenaries?" July 3, 2009.
"'Sorrow floats': The healthy-deregulated-capitalism myth just keeps resurfacing," September 10, 2009.
"In this era of incivility, messianic nationalism strides to the fore," September 21, 2010.
"Dealing with the prison of deregulated capitalism," February 12, 2010.

Thanks to Steven Shoemaker for copyright permission for use of all poems appearing in this collection.

In memory of Kosuke (Ko) Koyama
(1929–2009)

Gentle and strong, as trees
Bend gracefully in wind,
You stand—and I bow.

—Peggy Shriver, 2009

If we keep going the way we're going,
we're going to get where we're going.

—Navajo Wisdom

America is living stormy Monday,
but the pulpit is preaching happy Sunday.
The world is experiencing the Blues, and
pulpiteers are dispensing excessive doses
of non-prescription prosaic sermons with
several ecclesiastical and theological side-effects.
The church is becoming a place where
Christianity is nothing more than
Capitalism in drag.

—Otis Moss III, *Blue Note Preaching in a Post-Soul World*

He makes wars cease to the end of the earth;
he breaks the bow, and shatters the spear;
he burns the shields with fire.

"Be still, and know that I am God!
I am exalted among the nations,
I am exalted in the earth."

—Psalm 46:9–10

Contents

Foreword

by Eric Ringham

News Editor, Minnesota Public Radio

In any newsroom, there's a predictable pattern to the unfolding of a major story. First comes the initial, fragmentary report: a tsunami has struck, or there's been a school shooting.

Then there's a ghastly little pause, when it's clear that this story is indeed one of those awful ones, but there's a frustrating lack of material to publish. It can be a special problem for commentary and op-ed editors. That essay on France's burkini ban that we were planning to publish will seem aggressively off-point in the days after a terrorist attack.

Fortunately for me, there's been another dependable element of the pattern: the phone call from Gordon Stewart.

I couldn't begin to guess how many times I've heard his calm, deliberative voice on the line: "Hello, Eric? Gordon Stewart calling. I've sent something to your inbox."

That "something" would be an essay on exactly the topic of the hour—a nice, short (to an editor, "nice" and "short" are redundant) exploration of the moral aspect of the story. Sometimes he reaches into his personal history; sometimes he pointedly unpacks the fallacies that surround a public current event. The consistent characteristic of these essays is that he always addresses the moral or ethical element of an issue. If there is an angel in the room, he wrestles it.

I don't think I've ever told him how comforting his calls have been to me. Yes, he's a writer calling to pitch a commentary, but by the time the call has ended, I feel like a hospital patient who's just received a visit from the chaplain. In a word, I feel better.

Gordon knows something about writing commentaries that many people of faith do not: that is, how to be inclusive in addressing an audience that may hold some other faith, or no faith at all. He writes from a Christian perspective, but not to a Christian perspective. He writes to everybody.

I'm a different kind of editor now, and it's been a few years since I've been directly involved in publishing Gordon's work. I miss reading his commentaries, which is why this collection is such a pleasure.

In *Be Still! Departure from Collective Madness*, Gordon demonstrates his ability to be both topical and versatile, both insightful and unconventional. He ponders the manatee's knowledge of Disney World, the barbarity of beheadings (whether committed in the name of Allah or the Old Testament God), and the fate of a man just hours from his scheduled execution. He claims an affinity for John Lennon and admits his sympathy with Lennon's song "Imagine."

And there is much more, besides: the evils of Hitler, the remorse of a World War II Marine, gun control, the deaths of black men at the hands of police, hearing loss, the pleasures of solitude, and the demands made by cell phones.

He revisits his childhood and reflects on his own death. "Whatever lies on the other side of my years is beyond my mortal knowing," he confesses. I imagine that on the day he reaches the other side, he'll find a way to write about that, too.

This gentle, thoughtful writer deserves a wider audience, and I'm glad you've found him.

Eric Ringham
September 5, 2016

Preface

I invite you to look at this collection as a kind of photo album. Each snapshot focuses on a singular moment in real time.

Like the times on which these essays focus, the author's lens is set in time. It developed from the experiences of faith and doubt, hope and despair, sanity and madness, solitude and loneliness, stillness and frenzy, companionship and forlornness. I alternate between the quiet calm of the psalmist—"Be still, and know that I am God" (Ps 46)—and deep disquiet over the madness that fills the news, and me.

Throughout it all, my camera lens looks as much for what is left unsaid as for what's said. Willem Zuurdeeg's and Esther Swenson's work in analytical philosophy of religion taught me to look and listen for the governing convictions a speaker takes for granted, the bedrock underpinnings upon which a speaker depends. To be human is to die. And to die is to live with what Rudolf Otto called the *mysterium tremendum et fascinans,* the larger mystery that both causes us to tremble and that draws us irresistibly, the whence and whither of existence itself.

Elie Wiesel and Walter Brueggemann challenge the collective madness that often passes for sanity. But their insights into the depths of collective madness are anchored in the deep stillness of Psalm 46. Kosuke Koyama, to whom this book is dedicated, knew collective madness as a youth in Japan and again in his adopted home in the United States. Over lunch one day, he made a statement that added to how I look at the world. "There's only one sin," he said. "Exceptionalism." I've been thinking about that ever since in relation to the manifold ways in which this one sin manifests itself: religion, race, nation, gender, culture, and, finally, species exceptionalism.

Perhaps a picture of a moment in time with Kosuke will whet your appetite.

The day I'm remembering, Koyama was scheduled to deliver the inaugural address for a new speaker series in Chaska, a forty-minute drive from his home in downtown Minneapolis. Shortly after we left his apartment, the car broke down on the entrance ramp to the interstate. It just quit! Neither one of us had a phone. While I ran back to get help, frantic because we were going to be late, Ko stayed with the car. I had forgotten what Ko had written in *Three Mile an Hour God*:

> We lead today an efficient and speedy life. . . . There is great value in efficiency and speed. But let me make one observation. I find that God goes "slowly" in [God's] educational process. . . . "Forty Years in the Wilderness" points to [God's] basic educational philosophy. . . . God walks slowly because [God] is love.[1]

When the mechanic and I returned to the car, Ko was sitting in the passenger seat like the Buddha himself—calm, cool, and collected. I asked whether he was OK. He smiled and said, "Good meditation."

I hope in some way the still shots of *Be Still! Departure from Collective Madness* offer you an opportunity or two for a "good meditation."

1. Koyama, *Three Mile an Hour God*, 6–7.

Acknowledgments

Minnesota Public Radio (MPR) and MinnPost (minnpost.com) aired a number of these essays on *All Things Considered* or published them online. This collection would not exist without the All Things Considered former Producer Jeff Jones, who first welcomed a submission following the Nickel Mines school house massacre. Former assistant MPR News Editor Eric Ringham, whose gracious foreword appears here, encouraged continuing submissions for the commentary page. MinnPost Managing Editor Susan Albright rarely declined a request and, like Eric, offered a wise editor's pen that improved each essay.

Wipf & Stock has been a joy to work with, thanks to Administrative Assistant Brian Palmer and my editor, Assistant Managing Editor Matthew Wimer, who were a quick email or phone call away during the publishing process.

Professors Esther Cornelius Swenson's and Willem Zuurdeeg's collaborative work in the field of analytic philosophy of religion is the indelible ink in which *Be Still!* is written. Likewise, Kosuke Koyama's metaphorical theological method and observation that exceptionalism is humanity's one sin altered the lens through which I have come to see the world. Koyama's provocative statement is applied here to racial, cultural, religious, national, gender, and species forms of exceptionalism. Thanks to Mark Koyama for permission to include his late father's faithful testimonies to the reign of God in this collection.

Acknowledgments

Life is nothing without good friends. Carolyn Kidder and Mona Gustafson Affinito pored over every word, improving the text with valuable comments and the eyes of a copyeditor, although it was the final copyediting of Gillian Littlehale (Gilly Wright's Red Pen) who whipped the manuscript into final shape. Emily Hedges, Courtenay Martin, Austin Wu, and Dennis Aubrey encouraged me to believe writing and publishing were more than exercises in vanity. Steve Adams, Faith Ralston, Chuck Lieber, and old friends and seminary colleagues Wayne Boulton, Don Dempsey, Dale Hartwig, Harry Strong, Bob Young, and Steve Shoemaker have sustained me through thick and thin. After ten years of sharing our blog, *Views from the Edge*, Steve Shoemaker's verse and poetry appear in *Be Still!* Wayne Boulton, my seminary roommate—fellow Presbyterian teaching elder, scholar, author, faithful friend, and cheerleader—graciously consented to write the introduction for the book.

My deepest thanks goes to my spouse, Kay Stewart, who spent as many hours working on this project as her sometimes cranky, absentminded husband. This collection would not have made it to the publisher were it not for Kay's daily encouragement, patience, mercy, guidance, and extraordinary wisdom. Kay's good cheer over morning coffee and interruptions of obsession rescued the text and the author from solitary confinement. Every page has Kay's fingerprints all over it.

Last, but by no means least, is a group of men who would be shocked to find themselves mentioned anywhere but in a courtroom. "The Brothers of Opal Street," as they called themselves—eight black homeless former inmates of Eastern State Penitentiary in North Philadelphia—had a farewell conversation in late August 1962, with me, a naive nineteen-year-old church street outreach worker. As we sat on the stoop of a boarded up tenement on Opal Street, they said good-bye with the startling instruction not to return to the ghetto. "Go back to 'your people' and change things there. Only when things change there will there be hope for the people here." What they called "my people" were in the white western suburb of Philadelphia. I have come to believe that last day on Opal Street was its own kind of ordination. This book is in memory of them.

Introduction

by Wayne G. Boulton

I first met Gordon Stewart at a Christian seminary in Chicago. We were roommates and became fast friends. But I still remember missing much of what he said. This guy knew more about church than I did, about religion than I did, about philosophy than I did, and—above all—he knew much more about theology than I did.

And since my roommate was a winsome conversationalist even back then, there was no avoiding dialogue with Gordon about matters broadly intellectual and religious. The point of thinking was talking . . . as in *talking with*. If there is a single characteristic that marks Gordon Stewart to this day, it would be the same one I saw early on in seminary: a passion for engagement.

Shaped and formed over a lifetime, *Be Still!* has a pedigree. It is a book written in the tradition of *public theology.* Don't worry overmuch about the phrase. What sociologist Max Weber wrote about defining "the Protestant ethic" in his famed *The Protestant Ethic and the Spirit of Capitalism* (1905) applies in full to *Be Still!* as public theology: you will have grasped what the term means as you finish the book now in your hands.

To see clearly, to see clearly, to see clearly—such is the great impulse and drive you meet on each page. In the massive oil spill in the Gulf of Mexico years ago, how are we to see what really happened there? With noble manatees in Florida, how are we *homo sapiens* to grasp something of the mystery of what it is to be *other creatures with us* in our modern, capitalist society? As a boyish ruler in North Korea plays with weapons of mass destruction, what now has become of our "national system"? . . . system for what? As the number of oysters in Chesapeake Bay drops dramatically, what do we see or even what do we hear being *said* here?

Though the religious roots of this vision and struggle are sometimes hidden, the thrust is public theology through and through. By the late nineteenth century, Christianity had produced only two major social philosophies: medieval Catholicism and Calvinist Protestantism. Within this recent period, however, the modern social gospel movement originated and developed a third—namely Christian socialism.

As a great cloud of witnesses, the women and men surrounding this fine book are not difficult to bring to mind: Wendell Berry, Jane Addams, Cornel West, Walter Rauchenbusch, Reinhold Niebuhr, James Luther Adams, Dorothy Day, James Gustafson, Paul Tillich, Jim Wallis, and many others.

The movement is novel for its idea of *social salvation*. The leading direction has been that in order to make Christianity relevant to technological, nationalistic, and capitalist society, the church must recapture the utopian and revolutionary character of the faith . . . only in modern form. The church's mission, the movement has argued, should be social, i.e., to transform the structures of society in the direction of social justice.

So how do you do that? With special assistance from his professor Zuurdeeg and his teacher Swenson and his prophet Stringfellow, *Be Still!* is the Reverend Gordon C. Stewart's answer. Peppered with poems and allusions and metaphors, the essays in this book (Gordon calls them "photos") all strike me as *psalmic*. They aim at evoking the reader's imagination, and at putting her in touch with a source of mystery that can't be precisely defined, much less fully comprehended.

We recall that the Psalter—or book of Psalms—is composed of 150 psalms, and that therefore Psalm 46 as a discrete expression is not only the source of the book's title but is also deeply embedded in its larger book. The more I read and reflect on *Be Still!*'s "photos," the more I am convinced that Stewart's volume is one before it is many. Try grasping the book as a single sermon on a single text—Psalm 46, the passage known informally as "the Refuge Psalm."

> God is our refuge and strength, a very present help in trouble. Therefore we will not fear, though the earth should change, though the mountains shake in the heart of the sea; though its waters roar and foam, though the mountains tremble with its tumult. (Ps 46: 1–3)

Introduced first in Psalm 2 and repeated frequently throughout the Psalter, this seminal idea of taking refuge in God gathers unto itself themes at once basic to *Be Still!* and critical to the Psalter as a whole. The commanding idea of "happiness," for example—a notion that famously reappears in the Beatitudes (Matt 5:1–11)—is close to unintelligible apart from refuge. Happiness derives from living in complete dependence upon God rather than upon the self. "Happy are all those who take refuge in him" (Ps 2:11c).

The same is true for "righteousness" in the psalms, which is never primarily a moral category but a relational term. "The righteous" are never considered as morally superior persons whose good behavior lays some kind of obligation on God to reward them. On the contrary, the righteous are precisely the persons who take refuge, who acknowledge their fundamental dependence on God for life and for their future.

What Psalm 46 gives us, I believe, is what we find *Be Still!* echoing on every page, that is, the very opposite of positive thinking. Try this, the psalm says. To illustrate how powerful a help God can be in trouble, we should regularly imagine the absolute worst that can happen to us. Try the most awful hurricane, and a terrible earthquake (vv. 2–3). But truth be told: given the Near Eastern worldview, the psalmist has something even worse than this in mind! Mountains were both the foundations that anchored the dry land amidst watery chaos, *and* they held up the sky. So the world's absolute worst natural disaster would be for the mountains to shake (v. 2) or tremble (v. 3).

So here is how to approach *Be Still!* The book is in the psalm family. Approach it as a kind of spiritual exercise to be read in small doses. It was written to be taken in small doses. And discuss it with your friends.

Tide Pools and the Ocean

Therefore, I bend to thy resounding tides,
And list the echo of thy countless waves,
A lone disciple, if perchance, my soul
That poor shell-gatherer, on the shores of time,
May by thy lore instructed, learn of God.

—L. H. Sigourney (1850)[1]

As a boy I would spend hours lost in the magnificence of the tide pools that dotted the coast of Rockport, Massachusetts. Wading in the tide pools is still my favorite thing to do. The tide pools are filled with fresh seawater. They are the temporary homes that give shelter to the starfish, crabs, periwinkles, and sea anemones that are left there for a few hours at low tide.

Perhaps religion is like a tide pool, a small pool of ocean water that points us to the vast mystery of the ocean on which its life depends. The tide pools hold a few drops of a vast sea. They are filled with the ocean, but they are not the whole ocean. Their health depends on the eternal rolling of the tides to refresh them.

Wading in a tide pool, it's easy to lose track of time.

But there are other tide pools, far back from the water's edge, created by the unusually high waves of a storm. Unreachable by

1. Sigourney, "To the Ocean," in *Poems for the Sea.*

the normal daily tides that would refresh them, they are cut off from the ocean that gave them life. They are without oxygen, yellow, and covered by green-yellow slime. Their original beauty has left them to the flies.

Perhaps, like religion, the soul is like a tide pool.

Watching the news these days I feel the way the great preacher Harry Emerson Fosdick did when he put the question from his pulpit at the First Presbyterian Church in New York City, "Shall the fundamentalists win?"[2] Elsewhere, in "Dear Mr. Brown: Letters to a Person Perplexed About Religion," Fosdick wrote,

> Since when has the Pacific Ocean been poured into a pint cup, that the God of this vast universe should be fully comprehended in human words? When one considers the reach of the sea over the rim of the world; thinks of the depths that no eye can pierce . . . one dare not try to put these into a teacup. So God sweeps out beyond the reach of human symbols. At once so true and so inadequate are all our words.[3]

I can only take responsibility from within the tide pool of my Christian faith tradition. Muslim imams, like Minneapolis Imam Makram El-Amin, are doing the same in theirs. A news story in the *Star Tribune* quoted him as saying, "We will stand in unity against these attacks and the appalling killing of the diplomat who was there on a peaceful mission."[4] Every pastor, rabbi, and imam is called to do the same in the face of the torrent of toxins of the yellowed tide pool.

When any religious tradition mistakes its pool for the ocean itself, when it denies the existence of neighboring tide pools along the edges of Eternity, fundamentalism wins. Things turn yellow and nasty. Only the daily refreshment of the tides can keep the tide pools fresh. Otherwise, we watch the news, asking Fosdick's old question, praying that fundamentalism and fanaticism will not win, knowing that without the ocean tides, the tide pools will pass with time.

2. Fosdick, "Shall the Fundamentalists Win?" *Christian Work*, 716–22.
3. Miller, *Harry Emerson Fosdick*, 399; Fosdick, "Dear Mr. Brown."
4. French, "Minn. Muslims Denounce Attacks."

Stillness at Blue Spring

When words become unclear,
I shall focus with photographs.
When images become inadequate,
I shall be content with silence.

—Ansel Adams[1]

I don't belong here.

Walking the wooden path of Blue Spring State Park next to the clear shallow waters, I am a trespasser in the habitat of the West Indian Manatees who winter here. I walk among the sabal palms and nature's stillness disturbed only by the distant roar of an engine somewhere above and other tourists who have come to see the manatees inch their way forward into the hot spring where they pause, reverently it seems, over the opening from deep in the earth below. Blue Spring is a sacred place.

So gracefully does the Manatee approach the spring head, the deep hole through the limestone that pours 111 million gallons of water per day from deep below the earth's surface, enough for every resident of greater Orlando to drink fifty gallons of water a day. The manatee knows nothing of nearby Orlando. Nothing about Epcot or Disney World. Nothing of the Holy Land theme

1. Attributed to Adams in *AB Bookman's Weekly: For the Specialist Book World*, 3326.

park. Nothing of technology, malls, or vacations. She lives where she is . . . in this special place where she spends her winters to stay warm by the heated water of Blue Spring.

Her movements seem effortless, so fluid and gentle, like the water around her. Her huge flat tail, like a leaf fluttering in a soft breeze, inches her upstream toward the place where the earth is refreshed by the natural hot tub, before the water from deep below the surface cools as it flows downstream to replenish the river. Slowly, very slowly, she moves to the edge of the black oblong opening, this hole in the earth, the spring head, the epicenter of the green pool at the head of the river where she lives. Her tail stops moving. She stays very still and bows her head, like the Virgin Mary pondering the mystery of an ever-virginal Incarnation.

The trespassers get to see this. We can only see it if we push away the noisy culture we have brought to this place; push away the interruptions of a gathering crowd of people talking on cell phones, laughing, and loudly speaking to their fellow tourists as though they were at the mall, cruising past the mannequins in the shop windows or stopping by a town for an hour or two on a cruise. Instead, this is where the manatees live more naturally than we.

The manatees have no enemies. None but us, their human brothers and sisters, who, like the distant plane flying overhead, pay them and their endangered species and habitat little heed, except for the Florida State Department of Parks and Recreation, which watches over their slow recovery from human threat.

The pool of Blue Spring is its own kind of temple. A sacred place of the deepest silence where only those natural to this habitat belong. Today I was there, and the beauty of it deepened the sense of Incarnation: the sacredness of flesh and blood and water and algae and sabal palms and a natural quiet that mellows the soul, joining the manatee in taking a bow over the place deep below the surface from which the water flows.

A Joyful Resting Place in Time

I think there is nothing, not even crime,
more opposed to poetry, to philosophy, ay,
to life itself, than this incessant business.

—HENRY DAVID THOREAU[1]

I'm on vacation . . . in a pool . . . in the Florida sun . . . where I wished to be several days ago when back in frigid Minnesota. I'm here . . . but . . . not quite here. I'm moving forward to something even in the water . . . not standing still in this pool. I'm doing my prescribed water exercises. Not so much because I've chosen to do them, but because there's nothing else to do. I'm bored.

"Lift left knee. Extend arms. Pull arms to side as left knee goes down and right leg lifts. Keep abdomen tight. Keep neck and upper back muscles relaxed. Repeat."

I'm doing the exercises, but even in this pool, I think I have to be moving forward, advancing to the other side. One, two, three . . . eleven. I reach the other side of the pool. Turn, repeat to opposite side. Count steps to give sense of progress.

Even in the Florida sun in this quiet pool with no distractions, I seem to feel I must accomplish something. Be on my way to something. If I'm in the middle of the pool, I'm working to get

1. Thoreau "Life Without Principle." Originally presented as a speech titled "What Shall It Profit?" in Providence, Rhode Island on December 6, 1854.

to the other side. When I reach the far side, I turn and start pulling for the opposite side. Until the counting of strokes reaches one hundred. Then I change the exercise routine . . . and repeat . . . one, two, three, four, five . . . eleven, reach goal, turn, repeat until I count one hundred strokes.

I get out of the pool, dry off, take my place in the lounge chair. I'm having trouble just *being* here . . . alone . . . in the Florida sun . . . by a pool surrounded by palm trees and tropical birds. I turn on the MacBook Air, and as I do, I notice I am refusing to be here . . . where I really am . . . right now. My spirit insists that I am placeless.

A small gray lizard perches on the arm of the lounge chair next to mine. I look at it. It stares at me. The lizard's throat blows up like an orange balloon twice the size of its head. I move. The lizard scampers away. This is the place where the lizard lives. I do not. I am human, capable of being everywhere at any time, but homeless, scurrying like the lizard for a resting place.

I put down my passenger ticket to everywhere and nowhere—the MacBook Air—and reach over for the hard copy of *The Art of the Commonplace: The Agrarian Essays of Wendell Berry* I've brought for a quiet moment like this . . . a time to think . . . a time to seek perspective. I open to the Introduction by Norman Wirzba.

> Novalis, the German romantic poet and philosopher, once remarked that proper philosophizing is driven instinctively by the longing to be at home in the world, by the desire to bring to peace the restlessness that pervades much of human life.
>
> Our failure—as evidenced in flights to virtual worlds and the growing reliance on "life enhancing" drugs, antidepressants, antacids, and stress management techniques—suggests a pervasive unwillingness or inability to make this world a home, to find in our places and communities, our bodies and our work, a joyful resting place.[2]

2. Berry, *The Art of the Commonplace*, vii.

The closest I get to that resting place is my daily afternoon nap back in Minnesota. I am not alone in the nap. Maggie and Sebastian join me in the siesta. Maggie cuddles up close to my head while Sebastian rests against my thigh, reminding their cerebral, restless friend that I really am a creature in one place . . . at home . . . in the same time and space with them. If I am distracted when the time comes for the daily nap, Sebastian herds me upstairs. "Come on, Dad, it's nap time!" Like the lizard, Sebastian and Maggie are attuned to time and place, the angle of the sun, the rhythms of day and night and their location in space, while their Dad is racing around the world and the universe on his MacBook Air looking for a resting place when the resting place is right up those stairs.

We humans think we are an exceptional species, superior to the lizard who scampers down from the lounge chair and the West Highland White Terrier and the Shitzu-Bichon Frise. Yet we refuse to recognize our home within the limits of life itself . . . time and place . . . here in the garden, erasing all limits with the MacBook Air until . . . we become . . . like God.

Discontent with embodied existence and valuing little, we scurry away, not seeing, not touching, not hearing, not feeling anything much but one, two, three, four . . . eleven, on our way to nowhere in particular where perhaps the MacBook Air will take us vicariously to a joyful resting place . . . outside the reality of time-bound lizards and dogs . . . a delusional placeless place beyond dust to dust, ashes to ashes . . . and we miss the whole experience . . . on the way to someplace which is no place.

I want to learn to be in one place at one time. I want to live less anxiously. More present, one might say, to embodied life in this one spot where I really am . . . this one place . . . and find within it a joyful resting place in time.

The Man Who Loved Graves

When I was just a young and naive pastor,
an old man in the congregation
would always arrive long before the rest
of the people at the grave site. He'd shun
the funeral, but haunt the cemetery . . .
Standing by the open grave, he'd state
his opinion of the deceased and share
with me the type, style and brand of casket
he'd told his wife he wanted when he died.
As the morticians say, he "predeceased"
his spouse, and when we met to plan, she tried
to grant his wishes to the very last.
She blessed their common gravestone with her tears,
but smiled through life for many happy years . . .

—Steve Shoemaker[1]

My great-great-grandfather Isaac Andrews founded the Andrews Casket Company and Funeral Home next to the trout stream in Woodstock, Maine, more than two hundred fifty years ago. Isaac was a minister. Because there was no carpenter in town, he not only stood at the graves; he built pine boxes for those

1. Shoemaker, "The Man Who Loved Graves."

he buried. Over the course of time, the simple boxes became the caskets of the Andrews Casket Company and Funeral Home. You might say Isaac had a monopoly in those Maine woods.

Only recently did the Andrews property leave the family when Pete Andrews, my late mother's favorite cousin, sold it to some whippersnapper who just wanted to make a buck.

My mother used to chuckle as she recalled playing hide-and-seek with her siblings in and among the caskets at the casket factory. The property, including the land, the mill, the old homestead, the funeral home, and the trout stream that had belonged to the family all those years belongs to someone new . . . which means that it, like Garrison Keillor's Lake Woebegone, never really did belong to us and does not belong to them. It does not belong to time.

Last October, my brother Bob and I stood with my cousins at the open grave of my ninety-nine-year-old Aunt Gertrude—our one remaining Andrews elder. I recited from *The Book of Common Worship*, the prayer I have prayed a thousand times at the open grave, the one my friend Steve and I prayed as young, naive pastors—a prayer for the living that feeds me day and night until my lights go out. I wonder if Isaac Andrews did the same way those many years ago.

"O Lord, support us all the day long until the shadows lengthen, and the evening comes and the busy world is hushed, and the fever of life is over, and our work is done. Then, in your mercy, grant us a safe lodging, and a holy rest, and peace at the last."

Standing at Aunt Gertrude's grave, I am like the widow of the man who loved graves. I smile through tears for all the years, and take strange solace in knowing that I don't really "own" a thing.

Memorial Day and the Soldier's Helmet

As wounded men may limp through life,
so our war minds may not regain the balance
of their thoughts for decades.

—Frank Moore Colby[1]

Memorial Day once honored the fallen soldiers of the Civil War, both Union and Confederate soldiers. They called it Decoration Day, and they laid wreathes and flowers on the graves of the dead soldiers.

When I learned this in elementary school, it struck me as more than a little strange. My father had served as a Chaplain on Saipan. My father was a good guy. The people he went to war against—the Germans, the Japanese, and the Italians—were not. How strange to honor soldiers who fought against each other, heroes all, killing each other, especially when one side was good and the other was evil. It was more than a little confusing.

Decades later, I'm a pastor sitting in my office. It's Monday morning. A phone call comes from a seventy-something-year-old former Marine. He's a big man, what tough guys call "a man's man," a World War II decorated veteran, six-feet-two, two-hundred-fifty

1. Colby, "War Minds," in *The Colby Essays*, 15.

pounds of muscle, part of the invasion of Saipan in the South Pacific when he was seventeen.

"My wife's out of town. Can you come over tonight for a drink?"

I've never been to their home. I'm guessing he wants to talk about his marriage.

That evening, he welcomes me and takes my winter coat. He pours us each a Scotch. We sit down in the living room.

"You know, I'm not one of these peace guys. I stopped going to church for a couple of years, but something made me come back. I started to listen and I kept coming, and all this peace stuff and Jesus stuff started to get to me. It's been a long time now. That's why I called you. I need to confess before it's too late.

"I hate the Japs! I know I'm not supposed to call 'em 'Japs', but I hate them! I do. But I can't hate them anymore."

He gets up and walks over to the mantel above the huge stone fireplace.

"My wife has no idea what's in this box. I've never told her. I can't tell her. I don't want it anymore. I want this out of my house. I'm asking you to take it. I don't care what you do with it. I can't live with it anymore."

He takes the box down from the mantel, places it on the ottoman in front of me, and opens the locked box with a key. He is shaking now and crying.

"This poor bastard! I killed this [expletive] with my bare hands!"

His whole body shakes as, one by one, he removes the contents: a Japanese soldier's helmet, dog tags, a pistol, two eyeteeth, and a lock of hair from the Japanese soldier he killed in hand-to-hand combat during the American invasion of Saipan.

"All these years of hate. This poor bastard was just doing the same thing I was. He was just doing his duty to his country. How will God ever forgive me? I just want this stuff out of my house. I want it out of my life! How will God ever forgive me? I can't hate anymore. I can't."

We stand in the middle of his living room. I hold him like a baby: a grown man—a "man's man"—sobbing and shaking with guilt, sorrow, grief, the horror of it, hoping for relief.

I take the contents home. I give the gun to a friend, a former Marine who's a gun collector. I have no memory of what I did with the box or what remained of the Japanese soldier. Memory is like that. It was too personal. It was too hot.

So . . . today I observe Memorial Day by returning to the original sense of Decoration Day—a day to remember the fallen, all of them—but even more, to recommit to ending the collective madness of war itself. I remember the in-breaking of a sacred stillness: three men in a living room—two Americans and one dead Japanese—and pray for something better for us all.

Mysterium Tremendum

Little Boys with Toys

Man is unwilling to accept the limits of his thinking. It is this nonacceptance which lies at the root both of "needs" and "self-deceit." It is the unwillingness to accept the fact that our understanding cannot transcend the limits of experience which leads not only to self-deceit but also to presumption.

—Willem Zuurdeeg[1]

It's one thing to play with toys. It's something else when the toys are nuclear bombs and missiles.

Watching North Korea's young leader Kim Jong-un play with the possibility of nuclear holocaust, Rudolf Otto's idea of the *mysterium tremendum et fascinans,* the source of holy dread and attraction that sends shudders down the human spine, comes clearly into view.

In *The Idea of the Holy: An Inquiry into the Non-Rational Factor in the Idea of the Divine and its Relation to the Rational*[2],

1. Zuurdeeg, *Man Before Chaos,* 140.

2. Rudolf Otto's seminal work was first published in 1917 under the title *Das Heilige—Über das Irrationale in der Idee des Göttlichen und sein Verhältnis zum Rationalen* (English: *The Holy—On the Irrational in the Idea of the Divine*

Otto examines the dimension of human life that is non-rational—neither rational nor irrational. Otto calls it the "numinous"—the "non-rational, non-sensory experience or feeling whose primary and immediate object is outside the self"—the source of both holy dread and majesty and the foundation of all religion.

The experience of the *mysterium tremendum et fascinans*—a Latin phrase defying precise definition, roughly translated as "the fearful and fascinating mystery," is *sui generis*—a category all its own. This *mysterium* invokes the senses of vulnerability and wonder, death and awe, the tremor and fascination of the finite before the infinite, the shiver of what is mortal standing before the abyss of nothingness and the glory of the eternal. It is the reality at once terrifying and sublime behind, below, above, and beyond the human condition.

We are shaped by "the age of reason" and the deeply held belief in historical progress. Those who lived before the idea of progress became the dominant Western conviction and preoccupation were more directly in touch with the numinous—more present, less distracted, and perhaps, in that sense, saner. But there are times that call the belief in progress into question. Times when we stand as directly before the *mysterium tremendum et fascinans* as those who lived under the stars and slept in caves.

North Korea's young leader Kim Jong-un threatening the world with nuclear holocaust abruptly challenges the optimistic view that history is an upward course of inevitable progress. We tremble once again at the fearfulness of mortality, but this time it is the tremble at what our own hands have made in the name of progress—the power of extinction.

The power of death is enticing, a sin to which Robert Oppenheimer, the father of the atomic bomb, later confessed. The human will to power becomes evil when real soldiers, real nuclear bombs, real missiles, and real threats of destruction are mistaken for childhood toys and computer games where human folly can be erased by hitting a reset button.

---

and Its Relation to the Rational).

Looking at the young North Korean leader, psychiatrists might see an Oedipal complex, the son outdoing the father at the game of nuclear threat, the boy who played with matches, determined that if his father was afraid to light the fuse, he would step out from his father's shadow onto the stage of world power in a way the world would never forget. We are all children inside, for both good (remaining childlike) and ill (remaining childish).

But deeper and more encompassing than any Freudian analysis is Otto's *mysterium tremendum et fascinans.*

The philosophical-theological debates about modernism and postmodernism are interesting. They deserve attention. But neither modernism's rationalism nor postmodernism's deconstructionism is equipped to address the most basic reality underlying the human condition: the *mysterium tremendum et fascinans* and the horror of its demonic distortion in the shrinking of it by the madness of the human will to power.

Whenever we take the ultimate trembling and fascination of the self into our own hands, the world is put at risk. In the prehistoric world of our evolutionary ancestors, the consequences were limited to a neighbor's skull broken with a club. In the advanced species that has progressed from those primitive origins, we have fallen in love with our own toys of destruction. The technical achievements and manufactured mysteries have become deadly surrogates for the *mysterium tremendum et fascinans*, sending shudders down the spine in terror and in joy before what is Real.

Our time is perilously close to mass suicide. Unless and until we get it straight that I and we are not the center of the universe, the likes of Kim Jong-un—and his mirror opposites but like-minded opponents on this side of the Pacific—will hold us hostage to the madness that lurks in human goodness.

Progress isn't all it's cracked up to be. The ancient shudder of the creature—the human cry for help in the face of chaos and the heart's leap toward what is greater than the self or our social constructs—unmasks every illusion of grandeur in a world increasingly put at risk by little boys with toys.

Our Anxious Time

A toad can die of light!
Death is the common right
Of toads and men,—
Of earl and midge
The privilege.
Why swagger then?
The gnat's supremacy
Is large as thine.

—Emily Dickinson (1862)[1]

Ours is an anxious time, a fearful time, an insecure time. We feel it in our bellies.

Anxiety, fear, and insecurity were the subject of philosophical theologian Paul Tillich[2] and philosopher of religion Willem Zuurdeeg,[3] for whom the questions were passionate and all-

1. Dickinson, "A toad can die of light!"

2. Born and raised in Germany, Paul Johannes Tillich (1886–1965) was the first professor dismissed from his teaching position in 1933 for his outspoken criticism of the Nazi movement. At the invitation of Reinhold Niebuhr, he and his family moved to New York where Tillich joined the faculty of Union Theological Seminary.

3. Born and raised in the Netherlands in a family that served as part of the underground resistance to Hitler's pogrom, Willem Frederik Zuurdeeg

consuming over their lifetimes. Even so, they were not the best of friends.

Zuurdeeg was a critic of Tillich's attempts to create a philosophical-theological system. He saw every system as a flight from finitude and ambiguity into what he called an "Ordered World Home" that makes sense of, and defends against, the anxiety intrinsic to finitude. For Zuurdeeg, to be human is to be thrown into chaos, and every philosophy from Plato to Hegel to Tillich is "born of a cry"—the cry for help, for sense, for protection, for a security that lies beyond one's powers.

But rereading Tillich's *Systematic Theology* after perusing the morning news leads to the conclusion that Zuurdeeg and Tillich were very close, as is often the case between critics of one another. One thinks, for example, of Sigmund Freud and Carl Jung in a similar manner.

For all their differences, Zuurdeeg and Tillich were joined at the hip by their shared experience with madness in society and the demise of the once-trusted foundations of Western civilization. The rise of the German Third Reich led them to lifelong searches not only for answers but for the questions that might lead to insight into the existential situation that tilled the ground for the flowering of Hitler's collective madness, which threw the world headlong into chaos and destruction.

Tillich distinguishes between anxiety and fear. Fear has an object. We fear an enemy. We fear Iran; Iran fears us. Israel fears the Palestinians; the Palestinians fear the Israelis. "Objects are feared," said Tillich.

> A danger, a pain, an enemy, may be feared, but fear can be conquered by action. Anxiety cannot, for no finite being can conquer its finitude. Anxiety is always present, although often it is latent. Therefore, it can become manifest at any moment, even in situations where nothing is

(1906–1963) spent his life asking how Western civilization's most sophisticated culture (Germany), could fall so easily into the hands of a madman.

> to be feared . . . Anxiety is ontological; fear, psychological . . . Anxiety is the self-awareness of the finite self as finite.[4]

Anxiety is the self-awareness that we are mortal. We know a toad can die of light—death is the common right of toads and men—and that our supremacy is no greater than the gnat's. We are excluded from an infinite, imperishable future. We were born, and we will die, and we know it. Despite every flight into denial, we know it in our bones. We have no secure space and no secure time. "To be finite is to be insecure."[5] In the face of this insecurity, said Zuurdeeg, the individual and the human species seek "to establish their existence" in time and space, though we know we cannot secure it. The threat we experience in the second decade of the twenty-first century is the threat of nothingness. Politicians pander to it. Some preachers pander to it. Advertisers prey on it. They and we eat anxiety for breakfast, lunch, and dinner.

Again, Tillich, writing as if for our time, "The desire for security becomes dominant in special periods and in special social and psychological situations. Men create systems of security in order to protect their space. But they can only repress their anxiety; they cannot banish it, for this anxiety anticipates the final 'spacelessness' which is implied in finitude."[6]

I sip my coffee with Emily Dickinson aware of, and thankful for, this moment of finitude, determined that I will not turn over my anxiety to the hands of those who promise security from every fear. Emily, Willem, and Paul looked directly into the heart of human darkness and saw a light greater than the darkness, remembering that a toad can die of too much light! I want to live by the light of such humility, courage, and wisdom.

4. Tillich, *Systematic Theology*, 1:191–92.

5. Ibid., 195.

6. Ibid.

The Common Ground Beneath the Gun Debate

> Who can endure permanently
> Plato's uncertain, unsafe balance
> on the brink of the abyss of chaos?
>
> —WILLEM ZUURDEEG[1]

If ninety-nine percent of reality is perception, analytical philosopher Willem Zuurdeeg argued that perception is the expression of something deeper and far more powerful.

Zuurdeeg, author of *An Analytical Philosophy of Religion* and *Man Before Chaos: Philosophy Is Born in a Cry*, spent his life listening to human speech for what lay beneath the surface of the language.

Homo loquens ("man-who-speaks") is *homo convictus* ("man-who-is-convicted/convinced"), the creature who establishes her/his finite existence in time by powerful, unshakeable *convictors* who anchor us against the chaos.

What we often describe as irrational speech, is, in fact, "convictional language," the hidden power of which can only be understood by a kind of "situational analysis, i.e., the life "situation" (historical-convictional context) of the one who is speaking. Our

1. Zuurdeeg, *Man Before Chaos*, 44.

varying perceptions are determined by the less conscious hidden convictions of implicit needs and unquestioned cultural traditions.

What is missing in the national debate is public expression of the nonrational perceptions of the word "gun" and the unspoken convictions that shape our different perceptions.

We not only hear the word "gun" differently; we hear different things differently.

Until we come together to discuss what we hear when we hear the word—our nonrational (not unrational, as in opposed to reason, but nonrational, as in beneath the presumptions of reason) convictional worlds—the gun debate will be a shouting match that finds no common ground.

A simple exercise of word association demonstrates the difference.

Say the word "gun" and listen for what it evokes in the hearer. In the ears of some, the word means safety and protection. In the ears of others, it means without protection or threat.

But if we listen carefully to the apparently opposite responses, we discover a common ground they share: The threat of insecurity. The threat of chaos.

Whenever we hear a scream, something powerful is under assault. Chaos threatens. We cry out against the chaos. We cry out against death and extinction.

In *Man Before Chaos*, Zuurdeeg claims that, from its very beginning, Western culture has been bound up with a powerful dread of chaos. Even Plato's philosophy, argues Zuurdeeg, is born of a cry.

> Socrates has died. He himself does not fit very well into Athens' political life. He is naked and defenseless and is not ashamed of it. He has the courage to cry against chaos and for Being and Goodness. All this has been smothered by the comfortable, although often quarrelsome, classical and medieval philosophy and theology. Who can live by a cry? Who can stand to hear such disturbing noise? Clear and calm reasoning under the guidance of venerable old philosophical schools (or just as respectable church fathers) enables us to live, make

> church and civilization possible. Who can endure permanently Plato's uncertain, unsafe balance on the brink of the abyss of chaos? By what does a man live? By a cry? Claims? The careful and broad elaboration of philosophy? All of them?"[2]

In the current debate about guns, the life situations, cultural traditions, and life experiences of the hearers are "worlds" apart. Perhaps . . . perhaps . . . if we could find the space to listen more deeply to our different cries in the face of chaos, we would find the common ground of *homo convictus,* and move to something deeper than the shouting.

2. Ibid., 43–44.

Say the Word 'Freedom'

I may not be able to say all I think, but
I am not going to say anything I do not think.
And I would rather a thousand times be
a free soul in jail than a sycophant or
coward on the streets.

—Eugene V. Debs[1]

My hearing continues to get worse. In the soundproof booth of the hearing test, the audiologist asks me to repeat the words I hear . . .

"Say the word 'good.'"
"Wood."
"Say the word 'cold.'"
"Hold."
"Say the word 'gold.'"
"Goal."

1. Debs, "Statement to the Federal Court." Eugene V. Debs (1855–1926) delivered a Canton, Ohio, speech to the Ohio State Convention of the Socialist Party in opposition to American participation in World War I. He was convicted of treason and sentenced to ten years in federal prison. Debs was a founding member of the American Railway Union (ARU), which was famous for the Pullman Strike. President Warren G. Harding commuted his sentence in December 1921.

Say the Word 'Freedom'

It's not easy inheriting my mother's hearing loss. Getting the words wrong often separates me from normal conversation. But it also has its advantages. I listen more carefully, and the world of silence brings me to a deeper reflection about the words we hear every day.

I've begun to listen more carefully when the word "freedom" is used.

"Say the word 'free.'"

"Free," we say. And something deep within us hears the national anthem: "land of the free, and the home of the brave."

We Americans love freedom.

Future anthropologists will likely observe that freedom was the most treasured word in the American vocabulary. It is the most powerful word in our language.

No one understands this better than the handlers of political candidates. They know that the word evokes an unspoken reverence and that perceived threats to freedom alarm us and cause us to get back in the ranks of freedom's faithful. They know the nature of language and of word association.

"Say the word 'freedom,'" they say.

"Democracy."

"Say the word 'regulation.'"

"Socialist."

"Say the word 'socialist.'"

"Un-American."

"Say the word 'government.'"

"Enemy."

"Say the word 'American.'"

"Free."

Freedom stands alone in the American pantheon.

Ironically, in the hands of the unscrupulous, the word we associate with individual liberty can cause a collective stampede. It calls us from grazing freely in the pasture to joining a mindless herd.

We don't like heresy; we're afraid of being heretics like Eugene Debs, convicted of sedition in 1918 for exercising his constitutional right to freedom in a speech at Canton, Ohio. Sentenced to ten years in federal prison, he exercised his right to make one final plea to the court.

"Years ago," he said, "I recognized my kinship with all living things, and I made up my mind that I was not one bit better than the meanest of the earth. I said then, and I say now, that while there is a lower class, I am in it; while there is a criminal element, I am of it; while there is a soul in prison, I am not free."[2]

My hearing will continue to get worse. It will take me into a world of increasing silence. In a way, I wish the same for the rest of my countrymen. We could all use some time away from the word-association games.

2. See Debs, "Statement to the Federal Court of Cleveland, Ohio" on September 18, 1918, after being convicted of violating the Sedition Act.

Reframing the Gun Debate

We hold these truths to be self-evident,
that all men are created equal,
that they are endowed by their Creator
with certain unalienable Rights,
that among these are Life, Liberty
and the pursuit of Happiness.

—American Declaration of Independence

Today in America we continue to define, weigh, and measure these three "unalienable rights."

No matter whether the Declaration's principal author, Thomas Jefferson, and the Committee of Five of the Second Continental Congress assumed these three rights to be mutually compatible or whether they saw them in tension with each other, today in America there is little agreement about the meaning of, or the relations among, "Life, Liberty, and the pursuit of Happiness." Instead, we are locked in a heated debate about *one* of the three—liberty—as it pertains to the Second Amendment to the US Constitution, adopted in 1791.

Lost in the debate is the more reflective philosophical, moral, and religious pondering of the "unalienable rights," which in the eyes of Jefferson and the Congress were essential virtues of a new republic. Then, as now, the way we understand life, liberty, and the pursuit of happiness is shaped, to some extent, by different cultural experiences.

A NEW CULTURAL LANDSCAPE

At the time of the Declaration of Independence, the differences were often between northern and southern colonies. Today, the differences are still sectional, but perhaps even more, they are between rural and small town, urban and suburban cultures and settings.

Rural and small-town populations, especially those that plow the fields and grow their food (and some of ours), tend to view guns as instruments that support life and the pursuit of happiness. A gun is used for hunting, protecting the animals from coyotes, or skeet shooting. The rifle by the back door is part of rural life, not meant to be used on another human being except in the unlikely event of a burglary. The right to own and use a gun is a matter not only of liberty but also of life and the ability to pursue happiness. The gun is a family friend.

Urban populations, especially those living in densely populated centers with the high crime rates that accompany economic deprivation, see guns differently. Guns in these neighborhoods are not for hunting, protecting animals, or shooting coyotes. They are threats to life and the pursuit of happiness. The cities are divided between very wealthy, middle-class, and the economically impoverished neighborhoods where gunshots are heard while putting children to bed. Residents who can afford to leave for the suburbs to pursue happiness sometimes do.

Suburban populations are a blend of former rural and urban dwellers with native suburbanites. Some grew up on the farm or in small towns where there was little or no tension among the three unalienable rights. Some left the city in pursuit of happiness or in search of a safe place to live. Some, born and raised in the suburbs, can imagine neither the farm, the small town, nor the city as a preferred place to live. In the suburbs, it is a matter of some confusion and debate whether liberty, as in gun rights, supports or conflicts with life and the pursuit of happiness.

The National Sheriffs' Association, serving rural and small-town America, takes a conservative position on gun rights and gun control, while the National Association of Chiefs of Police and the International Association of Chiefs of Police, serving urban, small cities, and large suburban communities, call for improved gun-control legislation.

LOOKING FOR A PRODUCTIVE CONVERSATION

Although informed debate about the origins and intent of the Second Amendment is good and necessary, a preoccupation with the Second Amendment all but ensures the demise of a productive national conversation. We would do better to look earlier in our history to the Declaration of Independence, which defined the goals of a soon-to-be-born American republic. To this writer's knowledge, there has been little if any discussion of gun rights and regulation in the context of the three unalienable rights explicitly lifted up in the document we all celebrate on July 4.

Those who declared American independence from Great Britain in 1776 could not have imagined that one of the three named unalienable rights—liberty—would stand as the sole right without reference to life and the pursuit of happiness.

Few venues lend themselves to a mature discussion among rural, small town, urban, and suburban American experiences. In theory, the fifty state legislatures and the US Congress provide the forums for thoughtful discussion and the search for solutions by representatives of rural, urban, and suburban constituents. But in today's America, where representative government itself is often viewed with distrust and even fear, the likelihood of success is far less than the founders might have hoped.

Time to explore the creative tension among rights

Where and how, then, do we, the people—rural and small town, urban and suburban—citizens of the diverse country we all love, come together to discuss our life in light of the creative tension of the rights to life, liberty, and the pursuit of happiness in 2016?

In 2016 one could hardly say we in America are happy. In the light of current gun violence tragedies and our socio-political history, we might do well to remember the wisdom of Aristotle (384–322 BCE) to help guide citizens of a constitutional republic: "Happiness depends upon ourselves."

The Execution of Troy Davis

It is fairly obvious that those who are in favor of the death penalty have more affinity with assassins than those who do not.

—Rémy de Gourmont[1]

Tonight, September 21, 2011, at seven o'clock eastern standard time, the state of Georgia is scheduled to execute Troy Davis. Mr. Davis was convicted of shooting an off-duty police officer on the testimony of nine state witnesses, seven of whom have since recanted their testimonies.[2]

The United States, by all accounts the most religious nation of Western culture, is the only remaining Western nation that practices capital punishment.

1. Parrinder, *Dictionary of Religious & Spiritual Quotations*, 270. Rémy de Gourmont (1858–1915) was a French Symbolist poet, novelist, and influential critic. His approach to literature influenced twentieth-century poets Ezra Pound and T. S. Eliot.

2. "The case against him consisted entirely of witness testimony that contained inconsistencies even at the time of the trial. All but two of the state's non-police witnesses from the trial recanted or contradicted their testimony . . . [stating] in sworn affidavits that they were pressured or coerced by police into testifying or signing statements against Troy Davis." See Amnesty International, "I Am Troy Davis."

Ironically, some of capital punishment's most outspoken advocates are Christians who seem either not to know or who are willfully ignorant of the fact that Jesus of Nazareth was a first century Troy Davis—he was sentenced and executed by the Roman state. Of what we know about Jesus himself, this one fact is clear. The cross, which subsequently became the central symbol of the Christian Church, was an instrument of state torture and public execution. It was the first century's electric chair, gas chamber, and gurney for execution by lethal injection.

Tonight, unless there is some divine or human intervention, Troy Davis will die by lethal injection, a less torturous method of execution than electric chair or gas, according to the state of Georgia. Execution by lethal injection ends, it is argued, with a slight cough.

Criminal defense attorney Joe Margulies,[3] formerly a staff attorney at the Legal Rights Center in Minneapolis, knows differently. Joe had taken on the case of Texas death row prisoner Betty Beets,[4] convicted of murder without effective counsel. Joe handled her appeals as a *pro bono* attorney, traveling from Minneapolis, at his own expense, to the Huntsville, Texas penitentiary to visit with Betty and to strategize her appeals.

The day Betty was executed, Joe was there. Before they took her away to the execution chamber, Joe said to her, "Don't think about what they're doing. Just look up at me. I'll be there."

Joe took his place in the small room to the right of the execution chamber, looking down through the soundproof glass window. As they strapped Betty to the gurney and inserted the needle into her arm, Betty looked up at Joe. "I love you, Betty," said Joe. Betty smiled and said something back. In moments, her body shook in convulsion. "It was not a cough," said Joe. "It was more than a cough. It was a racking spasm."

3. Joseph Margulies is a civil rights attorney who subsequently became professor of law and government at Cornell University and author of *What Changed When Everything Changed: 9/11 and the Making of National Identity*, and *Guantánamo and the Abuse of Presidential Power*. The Cornell University faculty page describes his work: http://www.lawschool.cornell.edu/faculty/bio_joe_margulies.cfm.

4. White, "Texas Executes."

Among the only things that Betty Beets left behind was a stack of fifty-plus handwritten letters sent to Joe from her cell on death row. Her handwriting was childlike. So was the content. Betty's life had been no cakewalk. She had been raped at the age of five, suffered incest, sexual and physical abuse, and had been left brain damaged by a car accident. The appeal was based on the ineffectiveness of her counsel. The evidence of abuse was never introduced at trial and Betty's original court-appointed attorney withheld information from the court that would have served as compelling evidence against the state's case. Governor George W. Bush ordered the execution.

Another Republican governor, Illinois Governor George Ryan[5]—a former believer in the death penalty—suspended all further executions after sixteen death row inmates were exonerated of all guilt by the volunteer investigations of students and lawyers of the Innocence Project.[6] "Condemning the capital punishment system as fundamentally flawed and unfair," wrote Jodi Wilgoren, "Gov. George Ryan commuted all Illinois death sentences today to prison terms of life or less, the largest such emptying of death row in history." Without Governor Ryan's intervention, those sixteen wrongfully convicted men would have died at the hands of the state.

If the sentence of Troy Davis comes to conclusion tonight with death by lethal injection,[7] there will be a greater question than whether or not Troy Davis was guilty of the crime for which a jury convicted him. The question is about the religious and moral character of those who endorse capital punishment, some of whose faith has its origins in a first century CE public execution.

Like Betty Beets, Troy's execution will likely end with more than a cough, but the cries from the cross will be heard by those with ears to hear: "My God, my God, why have you forsaken me?" and "Father, forgive them, for they know not what they do!"

5. Wilgoren, "Citing the Issue of Fairness."

6. The Innocence Project exonerates the wrongly convicted through DNA testing and reforms the criminal justice system to prevent future injustices.

7. The state of Georgia executed Troy Davis on September 21, 2011.

Religion and Politics

Cain and Abel

Where is Abel, your brother?
The voice of your brother's blood
is crying out from the ground.

—GENESIS 4:9–10

Religion and politics: oil and water? The problem is that each stakes a claim for the same turf. They both attempt to answer the question of how to live together. The fact that religious creeds and political creeds stake claims leads some of us to separate them, not only as they are separated by the US Constitution, but by carving out different spaces on the same turf: one private/personal sphere (religion), the other the public/social sphere (politics). Religion says to politics: keep your hands off my private beliefs! Politics says to religion: keep your hands off public policy!

With the exception of adherents of the extreme right or left in religion or politics, most of us have had enough of religious or political fundamentalism. We're tired of explosive tirades and single-issue politics spawned by fundamentalist religion. We're equally tired of political power plays that dress up a political party (take your choice) as the incarnation of righteousness.

The US Constitution does a good thing when it insists that there be no established religion in this country. Looking back on the failed experiment of the Massachusetts Bay Colony's blending of religious creed and political authority, which resulted in the banishment of dissident Anne Hutchinson (1637),[1] the execution of Quaker Mary Dyer (1660),[2] and the Salem witch trials (1692–93),[3] the framers of our Constitution had every reason to protect the body politic from the tyranny of any religious majority.

FAITH, A VISION OF THE PEACEABLE SOCIETY

But even as I celebrate the antiestablishment provision of the Constitution, there is no way to separate faith and politics. It's impossible because faith is about more than the private/personal sphere—it's a vision of a peaceable society. Faith and politics live in the same territory every time the vexing questions appear regarding the public/social/economic/military ideas and beliefs that create public policy for good or for ill.

The three Abrahamic religions—Judaism, Islam, and Christianity—answer "yes" to the question, "Am I my brother's/sister's keeper?" Our three traditions refuse to confine religion to the vertical and the private. Faith is a living relationship with the Divine that expresses itself, according to Amos, Jesus, and Muhammad, primarily in the daily practice of keeping or caring for the neighbor. Jewish, Christian, and Islamic faiths are social as well as personal, public as well as private. While alms-giving and charitable giving are essential, they count for little without also addressing the public policies that set the fires that drive people into the arms

1. The court of the Massachusetts Bay Colony presiding judge, Governor John Winthrop, declared Anne Hutchinson a heretic "unfit for our society."

2. Mary Dyer's execution directly influences the Rhode Island Charter of 1663 granting liberty of conscience. She is widely regarded as the source of the First Amendment of the US Constitution.

3. The Salem witch trials charged, prosecuted, and tried more than two hundred residents of the Massachusetts Bay Colony accused of witchcraft ("the Devil's work"). Twenty defendants were executed publicly, among them fourteen women.

of charity. The Genesis story of Cain and Abel, humanity's children, strikes me as a place to focus the discussion. It is the bloody parable in whose ink humankind's history is written. In the original Hebrew text, the names are Kayin (from the root word "get") and Abel (meaning breath, puff, vapor).

The Genesis writer offers in these names two kinds of humanity. Abel ("Puff") knows he is a breath, a mortal, a vapor dependent on the breath. His offering finds favor in God's sight. Get's offering does not. In defiance of the ways of YHWH, Get (the anxious acquirer) takes matters into his own hands. He takes Puff out to the field and kills him. YHWH (the name beyond our ability to name) asks Cain where his brother is. Cain answers with a crafty question that still echoes down the centuries with war and bloodshed and religious hatred: "Am I my brother's keeper?"[4]

A CALL FROM THE NRA

While concentrating on the Cain and Abel story last Monday, my phone rang. The little window on the phone said "NRA."

"Mr. Stewart?"

"Yes."

"I'm calling for _______, president of the National Rifle Association, to invite you to participate in a survey with one simple question. It will take just a minute of your time. Mr._______ has an important message. When the message is finished, Mr. _______'s assistant will come on the line for the one-answer survey."

The message went something like this: "Right now the United Nations is meeting behind closed doors planning to ban all guns everywhere in the world. Even as I speak, they're planning behind closed doors to take away your freedom in this country. The United States is a sovereign country. We cannot allow a bunch of banana

4. Plaut, *The Torah*, 44. Hebrew scholar W. Gunther Plaut notes that "Abel" is translated "breath" in English, as well as in Psalm 144:4 ("Man is like a breath; his days are as a passing shadow") and in the Book of Job 7:16 ("My days are as a breath").

republic dictators to take away the American people's freedom to bear arms. If we let them succeed, it will be the end of the Second Amendment and the end of freedom in our own country."

Mr.________'s assistant came on the line to pose the survey's one "simple" question: "Mr. Stewart, do you think we should allow the United Nations and a bunch of banana republic dictators to take away our freedom?"

"May I ask how you got my name?"

"Yes, sir, you're in our database as an NRA member, a contributor, or as someone who believes in civil liberties."

"Well," I said, "I am an advocate for civil liberties."

"So, Mr. Stewart, would you like to answer the question?"

"You want me to answer a question that has only one answer, a question premised on demagoguery, fear, and lies? Give me a break."

"You've had your break! Have a nice day, Mr. Stewart!"

At that point, I wished I'd had a gun. In the name of Abel and all things good, I was becoming Cain.

THE WORK OF ALL RELIGION AND POLITICS

YHWH tells an angry Cain in the Genesis story that "sin is crouching at the door, and its urging is for you. But you must master it." It is this human leaning toward violence that humanity must overcome.

The story of humankind is Cain's story, the refusal to master this leaning toward violence. The long sweep of human history is the story of the slaying of our brother/sister because we have not mastered the beast that crouches inside ourselves. "I am not my brother's/sister's keeper." The sin—i.e., the refusal to take responsibility, the rebellion of separation and of slaying those from whom we cannot be separated—goes unmastered, slaying the neighbor. It comes hurling down the centuries of human development in the form of a rock, a caveman's club, a sling shot, a rifle, a handgun, a bazooka, an M-15, an airplane turned into a missile, a drone that kills innocent civilian victims whose blood, as in the Genesis story, "is crying out to Me (YHWH) from the ground." Abel's blood is the ink in which our story is written. Cain's story sets the stage for the work of all religion and politics worthy of their callings. It is the real story of the fall from natural grace held in common by Christians, Jews, and Muslims. It also holds the key to rewriting the story, not by claiming innocence, but by taking responsibility in a violent world.

For faith and for politics alike there is one overriding question: Am I my brother's keeper? Do my religion and my politics slay or keep my brother/my sister from deadly harm?

Are we willing to reclaim the earth as sacred turf—through responsible religion and responsible politics—until Abel's blood no longer cries out from the ground to a horrified God?

Idealism and Terror

Never before has the individual stood
so alone before the lie-making machine.
We used to wonder where war lived,
what it was that made it so vile.
And now we realize that we know where it lives,
that it is inside ourselves.

—ALBERT CAMUS[1]

When one thinks of idealism, Martin Luther King Jr. and Gandhi come to mind. Moral and spiritual giants who stand for ideals that make the world a better place. We think of idealism as good in the face of evil, and of ideals lifting us up, purifying life from its toxins. But there lies the fatal flaw in idealism.

George Will's *Washington Post* opinion piece, "A Murderer's Warped Idealism," looks afresh at idealism and evil, not just evil masquerading as goodness, but idealism as a source and form of evil itself.[2]

Will's commentary zooms in on Adolf Eichmann, executed at midnight in 1961, for his role in the German State's systematic extermination of six million Jews. During the trial in Jerusalem

1.. Camus, *Notebooks*, 141.

2. Will, "A Murderer's Warped Idealism."

Eichmann minimized his role in the Holocaust, presenting himself as a thoughtless functionary carrying out his superiors' orders.

Based on newly discovered writings by Eichmann that form the backbone of German philosopher Bettina Stangneth's book *Eichmann Before Jerusalem: The Unexamined Life of a Mass Murderer*, which refutes the earlier consensus of Eichmann as a willing functionary, Will writes,

> Before he donned his miniaturizing mask in Jerusalem, Eichmann proclaimed that he did what he did in the service of idealism. This supposedly "thoughtless" man's devotion to ideas was such that, Stangneth says, he "was still composing his last lines when they came to take him to the gallows."[3]

Eichmann and Hitler were not without ideas or ideals. They were not thoughtless. Nor were they irrational, as those who think that reason can save us believe. They were idealists who sought to lift up a super race, burning away the world's impurities as their deranged hearts conceived of them.

The late Dom Sebastian Moore, OSB, shed a similar light on idealism and the remedy for human madness. He put it this way in *The Crucified Jesus Is No Stranger*:

> We have to think of a God closer to our evil than we ever dare to be. We have to think of [God] not as standing at the end of the way we take when we run away from our evil in the search for good, but as taking hold of us in our evil, at the sore point which the whole idealistic thrust of man is concerned to avoid.[4]

We are, says Moore, "conscious animals scared of our animality and seeking to ennoble ourselves."

Eichmann, Himmler, and Hitler were idealists. Nationalist extremists are idealists. Racial and religious extremists are idealists. ISIL is idealist. American exceptionalism is idealist. Whether behind the banner of the State or of religion, gender, ideology,

3. Ibid.
4. Moore, *The Crucified Jesus Is No Stranger*, 47.

scientism, or rationalism, idealistic terrorism lives to rid the world of evil as its adherents understand it, projecting evil as "the other" while fleeing "the sore point" in ourselves that we conscious animals seek to avoid.

Only the God who meets us at the sore point of our shared animality can save us from the fantasies of exceptionalism. In his last book, *Remembered Bliss*, Dom Sebastian introduced the collection of poetry with a letter to the reader. The letter opens with this summary statement about his life: "I'm ninety-six, and for most of my life I've been a monk. My life as a monk has been, for the most part, the search for God as real."[5] RIP.

5. Moore, *Remembered Bliss*, v.

Being Human

Nothing Less and Nothing More

Threatened by nonbeing, by chaos,
and meaninglessness,
man looks for a foothold in the Imperishable.

—Willem Zuurdeeg[1]

The ISIL fundamentalist extremists who terrorized Paris, San Bernardino, Beirut, and elsewhere in the name of God believe in an eternal reward for sacrificing themselves for a holy cause. Though it may seem strange to many of us in the West, they share two widely held beliefs:

1. God is 'a being'—the *Supreme* Being, but 'a being' nonetheless.
2. Death is not the end of life; we are destined for immortality—heaven or hell, eternal states of bliss or punishment.

The "soldiers of the caliphate" are young. Paradoxically, as mad, hideous, grotesque, and deranged as their thinking is, their massacres are performed in the name of an ideal. They are idealists claiming "a foothold in the Imperishable."

Seeking to rid the world of evil, they succumb to evil. In the name of heaven and the imperishable, they create hell on earth.

1.. Zuurdeeg, *Man Before Chaos*, 79.

But it's not just the jihadist extremists who deny our mortality, our perishable nature within the order of Nature.

But what if God is not a being? What if, as Paul Tillich argued, God does not "exist" as a thing or person exists, but instead is Being-Itself or the Ground of Being or the God above god?

What if we are mortal? What if death is the end, not a doorway to heavenly reward or eternal punishment? What if no St. Peter stands at the pearly gates to separate sheep and goats? What if no vestal virgins are waiting? What if life and death are what they seem?

John Lennon's "Imagine" strikes a chord in the aftermath of the attacks in Paris, Beirut, and Mali. Imagine there's no religion. But imagining won't erase the problem of religion or the anxiety endemic to the human condition. We are easy prey, desiring the end of complexity and ambiguity.

"Finitude," wrote Paul Tillich, "means having no definite place; it means having to lose every place finally, and with it, to lose being itself."[2]

The appeal of fundamentalist certainty, whatever its form, is the promise of a secure foothold, a place in immortality—a purpose bigger than life itself, the escape from ambiguity.

When faith is ill conceived, acting to end the ambiguities represented by the enemies of God instead of coping with life's inherent ambiguities, we create what we seek to escape. We create a foothold in what will not hold.

What if to be human is not to escape mortality, but to embrace it thankfully and to live courageously within the boundaries of time, of mortal flesh filled with the Eternal in the midst of time?

> Being holy . . . does not mean being perfect but being whole; it does not mean being exceptionally religious or being religious at all; it means being liberated from religiosity and religious pietism of any sort; it does not mean being morally better, it means being exemplary; it does not mean being godly, but rather being truly human.[3]

2. Tillich, *Systematic Theology*, 1:195.
3. Stringfellow, *An Ethic for Christians*, 311–12.

Creating Hell in the Name of Heaven

Sin may take other forms, of course, but for Luther
the tragedy of sin is finally and preeminently a religious tragedy.
[Sin] is idolatry, not atheism or brute profanity . . . It is perverted praise,
misdirected glory, self-bestowed,
and disastrously and "deeply curved in upon itself."

—Matthew Myer Boulton[1]

The bombings were felt in my living room last night.

The horror of the suicide bombing of a church in Pakistan that killed eighty people echoed in the voices of two Pakistani members of Shepherd of the Hill Presbyterian Church in Chaska, Minnesota, where I serve as pastor. Twelve members of the church had gathered to talk about something totally unrelated to Pakistan, Afghanistan, or Christianity and Islam. We were there to share. The quiet horror of Samuel and Nasrin—"I was sad all day," said Nasrin—was like a bomb going off in the living room. I asked myself then, Why? What is happening? I ask it still.

I am a Christian, a disciple of Jesus. Strange as it may seem, I often feel the way John Lennon did. I dream of a different kind of world where there are no bombings or shootings in a Kenyan

1. Boulton, *God Against Religion*, 162–63.

mall, in the Pakistani cities of Peshawar and Lahore, in Baghdad, Damascus, or Boston in the name of God. I am tired of all claims to righteousness, whether professedly religious or professedly secular. I would like to wipe the human GPS of its magnetic field between due north (heaven) and due south (hell) and reorient us all toward the rising sun.

The voices that fight for heaven to erase hell do not all sound the same. They speak Urdu, Parsi, Arabic, Hebrew, and English. They claim different names: Muslim, Jewish, Christian, and sometimes secular. They live in different parts of the planet in different time zones and different climates. But if you listen, they all sound alike and they do the same thing.

They do not look up at the sky. They look down. They march in lockstep rhythm because the Koran or the Bible or some "ism" tells them to. They live for tomorrow—for heaven or some version of it—not for today. One doesn't have to strain to see what's happening, and, when anyone sees it, how can one help but imagine a different world, a different kind of humanity—one without religion?

The bombing in Peshawar last Sunday is said to have been payback for American drone strikes that killed innocent civilians in Pakistan. For the suicide bombers, the cross was the emblem on the shields and helmets of Christian Crusaders. Back then the Knights Templar of Holy War killed with swords. Today the suicide bombers associate the cross with the drone attacks of the Christian West.

Religion is with us and, depending on how one defines it, always will be. A wise elder statesman, Elliot Richardson, observed toward the end of his life that religion is the problem, but that if we erased all of the religions from the face of the earth, they would reinvent themselves in a heartbeat. Why? Because that's how we're made. As defined by the likes of Emile Durkheim, Margaret Meade, Mircea Eliade, and Paul Tillich, religion spans a much wider terrain than the belief systems for which heaven and hell are essential. Furthermore, whether or not we are professedly religious, each of us has some kind of inner GPS, some version of a societal ideal (heaven) and a social and personal horror (hell).

What's happening across the world is profoundly and earth-shakingly religious. Though our languages are as different as Arabic is from English, and as far from each other as Peshawar and a mall in Kenya are from a Koran-burning church in Florida, the voices of Abraham's three children (Judaism, Christianity, and Islam) all sound the same whenever we create hell on earth in the name of heaven.

For the Pakistani friends in my living room last night the cross stands for a divine interruption of the cycle of violence and all claims to righteousness. In the crucifixion of a Palestinian Jew in the first century CE, what we see is the antithesis of a crusade to eliminate hell in the name of heaven. On the contrary, the Jesus we seek to follow threw his life into the spokes of the wheel of violence to stop it, and we must do the same.

When the bombs tear through a church or a mosque or a neighborhood in the name of our imagined heaven for the righteous, we need to remember that there are Muslims, Jews, Christians, other religious practitioners, and secularists who seek to practice the way of peace, "living for today," throwing themselves into the spokes of the wheel of violence.

Losing Our Heads

The sheer arrogance of the idolatrous claims of nations, perhaps especially those possessed of enormous economic and military strength, is so startling that the fascination of men with such idolatry can be explained in no other conceivable manner than as moral insanity.

—William Stringfellow[1]

When Lewis Carroll wrote *Alice's Adventures in Wonderland*, he knew nothing about ISIS. But he knew about collective madness and the insanity of power in the high places of his own culture. In Disney's film adaptation of *Alice in Wonderland*,[2] the Queen of Hearts asks, "Who's been painting my roses red? WHO'S BEEN PAINTING MY ROSES RED? / Who dares to taint / With vulgar paint / The royal flower bed? / For painting my roses red / Someone will lose his head."

The Card Painter responds, "Oh no, Your Majesty, please! It's all 'his' fault!" The Ace blames the Deuce. The Deuce blames the Three. The Queen explodes.

1. Stringfellow, *Imposters of God*, 48.

2. *Alice in Wonderland.*

"That's enough! Off with their heads! I warn you, child . . . if I lose my temper, you lose your head! Understand?"

It is hard to imagine a more horrifying spectacle than what we have recently seen of Western journalists losing their heads in the Middle East. The fact that British and American citizens have joined ISIL is nearly as chilling as the killings themselves. We ask why one of us would dare "to taint with vulgar paint the royal flower bed."

There is no excuse for a beheading. It makes no difference if it's at the hands of ISIS or David, the hero of Judeo-Christian tradition who beheaded Goliath, or those who sought to demonstrate their zealous support for David, sneaking into the bedroom of Ish-bosheth, the son of Saul, to behead him and present his head to David at Hebron (2 Sam 4:9–13).

To their great surprise, David, the beheader of Goliath, is not pleased.

> "[W]hen wicked men have killed a righteous man in his own house on his bed, shall I not now require his blood at your hand and destroy you from the earth?" And David commanded his young men, and they killed them and cut off their hands and feet and hanged them beside the pool at Hebron. But they took the head of Ish-bosheth and buried it in the tomb of Abner at Hebron. (2 Sam 4:5–12)

We don't hear readings like that in church. But you will hear such Scriptures read daily in a Benedictine abbey, as I did while visiting Saint John's Abbey to get my own head and heart straight in anticipation of the death of my stepdaughter. The reading I'm remembering was just as ghastly as the beheadings of Goliath and Ish-bosheth and David's response ordering that Ish-bosheth's killers be killed and mutilated on the public square for all to see.

"Why," I asked my Benedictine spiritual guide, "do you read those readings? They're horrible!"

It would take too long to explain, he said, but, in essence, such stories are lifted up in the Benedictine daily worship because that sordid history—that capacity for violence and brutality—is a part of us still. We must never forget.

The pictures and stories of the ISIL beheadings are meant to terrorize ISIL's opposition in Syria, Iraq, Europe, and the United States. But they also produce a widespread determination to stop ISIL before it's too late.

"That's enough! Off with their heads! I warn you, ISIL . . . if I lose my temper, you lose your head! Understand?"

Moral outrage is in order.

Yet a friend asked a question I didn't want to hear and could not answer: "As grizzly as the beheadings are," he asked, "what's the difference between that and blowing people's heads off—enemies and children who are 'collateral damage'—with bombs dropped by a drone?"

No one knows what to do in the face of ISIL's expanding threat. Answers do not come easily. There are no "good" answers. Power will be and should be used. But before going too far down the road of exercising Western military power in ways that have produced hatred in the past and will undercut whatever consensus of moral outrage has developed toward ISIL, the monks at the Abbey remind us of the brutal response of David, whose beheading of Goliath at Hebron and parading of Goliath's head through Jerusalem preceded and surpassed the wrongful beheading of Ish-bosheth.

Like the Benedictine brother said, we must not forget our history. Otherwise we paint the roses red and we *all* lose our heads.

Two Kinds of Religion

Religion either makes men
wise and virtuous or it makes them
set up false pretenses to both.

—William Hazlitt (1817)[1]

Everyone from time to time feels insignificant, as I did while watching fires burn across the world, lit by the words of one pastor in Florida. I felt like a spectator in the stands watching a game I care about go terribly wrong, a hostage of verbal terrorism uttered in the name of Christ.

I would imagine that Rev. Terry Jones's small congregation had also felt insignificant before they announced the 9/11 Koran burning, and that they were stunned when their pastor's voice, although terribly misguided, lit the forest on fire without ever burning a Koran. One of their own, one who had felt insignificant, had raised his voice and now had the ear of a commanding general, the secretary of defense and the president of the United States.

The difference between Rev. Jones and most people is that he has a pulpit. On any given Sunday he speaks and a few people actually listen. Most of us do our ranting and raving in the shower,

1. Hazlitt, *The Round Table*, 192. William Hazlitt (1778–1830) was an English writer, painter, social commentator, and philosopher.

at the water cooler, or with like-minded people at the coffee shop, but we don't much expect anyone else to listen.

But as the Jones story developed, those of us with pulpits were feeling insignificant ourselves. Then, as I prepared for worship, I was drawn by some old lines about spiritual arson. "How great a forest is set ablaze by a small fire! And the tongue is a fire . . . a restless evil, full of deadly poison. . . . And a harvest of righteousness is sown in peace for those who make peace" (Jas 3:5–8, 18).

The thought crossed my mind: I could invite a Muslim friend to join me in the pulpit, perhaps my neighbor Muhammad or Abdi or one of their children, whom I meet daily while walking the dogs. I decided to invite Ghafar Lakanwal, a Pashtun Afghan-American cultural diversity trainer, a Muslim and naturalized US citizen, to bring greetings of peace and share some passages about peacemaking from the Koran in our Sunday worship on September 12.

Our little church in Chaska welcomed Ghafar, and his words about the spiritual "obligation to learn, not burn" still ring in our ears. Our service drew media attention, and Ghafar's words were heard on the evening news and noticed by a stranger in Australia, who sent a message through the church website. "I was touched," he wrote, "when I read about your recent Sunday service in the news . . . I, for one, can testify that it has certainly comforted a faraway Muslim to know that there are neighbors who will stand together in difficult times. My salaam to you. May we all grow together to attain Allah's pleasure."

"Ah!" someone will say. How can any Christian rejoice when the author uses the name "Allah" for God? But the reaction is symptomatic of a misunderstanding. "Allah" is not a name. It is the Arabic word for what we in English call God. The forest fire lit in defense of "God" in advance of the anniversary of 9/11 reminds us that two kinds of religion potentially exist everywhere people gather to practice their faith. One kind burns. The other kind learns. One hates; the other loves.

As James, writing to those who would follow Jesus, put it: "With [the tongue] we bless the Lord and Father, and with it we curse those who are made in the likeness of God. From the same mouth come blessing and cursing. My brothers and sisters, this ought not to be so" (Jas 3:9–10).

We can set the forest ablaze with our small spark or we can use it to light a candle of hope and peace. But, after the events of this month, none of us can again think that what we say is insignificant.

A Visit to South Paris

wanting everyone to know
just how great we are
or denying to ourselves
and to everyone else
that we have skills and smarts
that could win 10,000 hearts
treating others as beneath
us or even inhuman
being irresponsible
for myself or for the world
worse is not caring at all
being dead before we fall
finally into our graves
death is God's last enemy

—STEVE SHOEMAKER[1]

I never met Bunny Benson. But I saw him many times. His name is etched in my mind from childhood.

Every summer my family would pack up the car and head for South Paris, Maine. We had little money, so we made the long

1. Shoemaker, "What We Are Supposed to Hate."

trip from Philadelphia to spend two weeks of vacation with the grandparents, aunts, uncles, and cousins in Maine. While my schoolmates ventured off to national monuments and resorts, the Stewart family vacation was an immersion in the culture of South Paris—and a lesson in how society works.

Bunny was a key figure in how things worked in South Paris.

Remember the story of the Good Samaritan? Bunny Benson wasn't the Good Samaritan. He was the man lying in the ditch.

I was eight years old the first time I saw Bunny. It frightened me. Driving past the scene in the back seat of my uncle's fancy new Kaiser sedan, I spotted him lying there alone by the side of the road.

"Uncle Bob, there's a man in the ditch back there. He needs help!"

My uncle shook his head with some compassion, but we didn't stop.

"Is he dead?" I asked.

My cousin Dennis, who knew what everyone else in South Paris knew, started to laugh. "Oh, that's just Bunny Benson. He's a bum. He's the town drunk."

Bunny was no stranger to my cousin—or to my uncle Bob. My uncle was the judge in town. First in his class at Harvard Law, he could have gone anywhere in the country. But he didn't. He set up a law practice in South Paris, bought a house on Porter Street, and went on to became the judge of Oxford County. Uncle Bob was a community icon of spiritual and moral virtue; Benny was the icon of spiritual failure and moral depravity.

And that's how I understood the world. Until the day my cousin and I ventured into the basement of the house on Porter Street. We found a six-pack of beer in the downstairs refrigerator—and then a couple of cartons of empty beer bottles. Dennis was horrified. "I didn't know my father was a drinkin' man!" he said to my aunt Gertrude. Most of the drinking in South Paris went on behind closed doors and pulled drapes.

The beer was Uncle Bob's. I learned years later that my grandfather, married to a loyal member of the Women's Christian

Temperance Union, would sneak over to the house on Porter Street to have a little port or sherry most nights after dinner. He would tell Eva he was going "for a little visit" with Gertrude and Bob. My grandmother never knew. But Uncle Bob and Aunt Gertrude sure did . . . and they never said a word.

There were two societies in South Paris. One public, the other private. One in the gutter, the other behind pulled drapes.

In all the years that I drove by Bunny lying by the roadside, I couldn't figure out for the life of me how we could revere the story of the Good Samaritan and still pass by like the priest and the Levite in Jesus's parable. It confused me. Until the day I realized that the people of South Paris needed Bunny more than Bunny needed them. They needed someone to play the role of the community scapegoat—the moral outsider—whose assigned role in town was to make everybody else feel good about themselves.

As long as we have a Bunny, we get to feel superior. We can point to him to define what we are not. When I was a child, we could point to Bunny as the bum. Later, we pointed to the communist, the atheist—the unbelieving spiritual and moral degenerates. Now we point to "the Jihadist terrorist" to define what we are not. Bunny is still the most important guy in town. He brings us all together. And we never have to deal with who we are behind the pulled drapes of our own house. We get to hide what's in our own basement.

Meeting the Boogie Man

We have nothing to fear
but fear itself . . .
and, of course, the boogieman.

—Pat Paulsen[1]

The Boogie Man lived in the cellar of the house on Hobart Road in Chestnut Hill, right across the street from Boston College, where I lived while my father was serving in World War II. My cousin Gina, nine years older, also lived in the big house with my mother and our grandparents.

It was Gina who told me about the Boogie Man. I never saw him, but I knew he was real. Gina said so, and I loved and trusted Gina. The Boogie Man would get us, if we didn't watch out.

No one ever sees the Boogie Man. He stays hidden in the basement. He lurks in your bedroom closet or hides under your bed. He's waiting just outside the door. Or maybe he's standing right there in front of you. You can't tell because he's invisible.

As a white child of relative privilege, I imagined what the Boogie Man looked like. Sometimes, sitting around the dining room table listening to the radio, we would hear the voice of Adolf

1. Emmy Award-winning comedian Pat Paulsen (1927–1997) ran satirical campaigns for president beginning in 1968 on *The Smothers Brothers Comedy Hour*."

Hitler. Fear and anxiety filled the room every time his voice was heard or his name was mentioned. Maybe my father had gone off to kill the Boogie Man so he wouldn't come to our house. The Boogie Man must be German. Or Japanese. Other times, listening to my cousin, I was convinced that the Boogie Man must be "colored," as she would say.

The first time I thought I saw the Boogie Man, he was driving a dump truck. My five-year-old friend Teddy Bonsall and I were playing dangerously near the street, and he honked at us. We looked up, saw that a black man was driving the truck, ran all the way to Teddy's house, raced up the stairs to Teddy's bedroom, and bolted the door. We told Mrs. Bonsall that the Boogie Man was after us.

After my father defeated Hitler's fascists and the Japanese imperialists, the Boogie Man became a Communist. I would watch newscasts of the Chinese Red Army marching into Korea to spread communism and take away democracy and freedom. We were at war with the Boogie Man.

In elementary school, we regularly practiced protecting ourselves from a threatened nuclear attack by the Soviet Union. At the sound of the school alarm—the stand-in for an air raid siren—we all dove under our desks. Even in elementary school, I knew that a wooden desk wouldn't protect me from a nuclear firestorm, but the drill succeeded in drilling into our young hearts the fear, the dread of the Boogie Man.

Beyond the regular drills that reminded us of the Boogie Man in Korea, China, and the Soviet Union, I learned that he might be in my own backyard or, as Gina suggested, in the closet of my own house.

I would race home from school to watch the televised US Senate hearings during which Wisconsin's Senator Joseph McCarthy used innuendo and slander to ruin people's reputations and careers, looking under the beds and in the closets for suspected Communists or Communist sympathizers who would take away our freedom. We began to wonder about each other's parents.

I'm older now, but I know the Boogie Man is real. He exists on the food of my psyche. He eats anxiety for breakfast and mortal fear for dinner. He sits invisibly at our tables and our televisions as we listen to the evening news. The more anxiety we serve up, the bigger he grows. He thrives on the terrorized heart—the threat of nothingness, the fact of our mortal vulnerability. He grows bigger and more dangerous when cultures and economies become insecure and need someone to blame. He lives in the collective unconscious that projects its invisible fears onto a tangible target. Nobody ever sees the Boogie Man, but we spend our lives looking for him.

For my generation, then, he was the different-looking person who sent us running to a friend's house. He was the voice and face of Hitler and the goose-stepping Nazi storm troopers. He was the Kamikaze pilot sacrificing his life for the Japanese empire. He was the Chinese soldier marching into Korea to steal freedom from the world. He was the Soviet Communist who made us dive under our desks in school and look in our closets to see whether Joe McCarthy was right.

Today, I see evidence of the Boogie Man in strange places. I hear again the shrill voice of McCarthy shouting and screaming about government, communism, fascism, and socialism, demonizing efforts to provide universal health care as a conspiracy, a plot to take away individual freedom.

I've seen the Boogie Man's terror in the murder of a part-time US census worker hanging from a tree alone in a dark forest with the word "Fed" scrawled on his naked chest. Now I've seen it on the bumper of a big new Mercedes-Benz ahead of me at the stop light with a sticker equating President Obama with communism. A black president with a suspicious name who sees government as part of the solution in a time of national crisis gets stuck on a bumper sticker as the new Boogie Man who's going to take away your Mercedes—or the Mercedes you wish you had but will never afford.

Watching the news these days, I feel the way I did back when the dinner table in Chestnut Hill was laden with the food that fed the Boogie Man. I grow more anxious every day, not because of the Boogie Man, but because we seem so hell-bent on feeding him at our own expense.

The Waiting Room

If all our time is present time to God,
our moans and screams of rage are heard not in
the quiet of primordial time, but heard
right now—just as we feel the blaze of pain
ourselves. So in cacophony of grunts,
of cries and whispers, gasps, expiring sighs,
our tiniest mew cuts through and joins the dance
of horror in the mind of God. The days
we suffer isolated from the world . . .
the hours of rejection, perfidy,
and lies . . . the minutes, seconds, that we bleed
from the real steel of surgeon, soldier . . . are shared.
We cry we are forsaken—our cry is heard;
Our tears run rivers down the face of God.

—Steve Shoemaker[1]

The surgery has gone "as well as could be expected" after two months of undiagnosed illness, but sepsis is taking over his body, threatening his survival. The next two hours are critical.

1. Shoemaker, "Cries and Whispers."

His loved ones and friends are gathered in the surgical intensive waiting room at Abbott-Northwestern Hospital in Minneapolis.

At sundown, several hours earlier, I observed six men praying the Muslim evening prayer at the far side of the waiting room. The men, who I assumed to be Somali, proved to be Oromo. They are gathered now in chairs in the center of the waiting room, talking among themselves in their native tongue.

When I approach them, intruding into their space, they acknowledge my presence. They stop talking.

"Salaam," I say.

"Salaam," they respond, as if with a single voice and smile.

"My friend is very sick. The next two hours are critical. I ask your prayers. His name is Phil."

They respond as one would expect compassionate people to respond. "We will pray for him."

I return to the small family area where my fellow Christians are gathered. I tell them the Muslims are praying for Phil. They're pleased. We chat. Phil and Faith's pastor eventually leads us in a Christian prayer.

An hour or so later, three of the Oromo men come to our little room. They have come to tell us they have finished their prayers for Phil. Led by their imam, the men's voices and eyes are kind, pastoral, as we say in the church. Full of compassion and concern. They have prayed in Arabic a Muslim prayer for healing on behalf of a stranger about whom they know nothing but his need:

"Remove the harm, O Lord of humankind and heal [Phil], for You are the Healer and there is no healing except Your healing, with a healing which does not leave any disease behind."[2]

Sometimes we have no choice but to wait. The Muslim Oromo friends are waiting with us actively. Would that we all would wait so kindly, so patiently, so actively, so humbly, so prayerfully, so wisely.

For a split second, I imagine the world as a waiting room.

2. http://www.duasfor.com/islamic-dua-for-good-health/

Jesus in the Hospital

> When I catch myself resenting not being immortal,
> I pull myself up short by asking whether I should really
> like the prospect of having to make out an annual
> income-tax return for an infinite number of years ahead.
>
> —Arnold Toynbee[1]

I had one of those nocturnal throwback dreams people sometimes have.

It's a Sunday morning. I'm the senior minister just returned from being out of town. The other ministerial staff and I are robing for worship. Though I'm the preacher for the morning, I am totally unprepared. In addition, I remember that we are scheduled to receive new members from the new members' class during worship. I ask Byron, the wonderful real-life former colleague who shows up in the dream, for an update. Byron is clueless. He fears the members of the class haven't been notified. Perhaps no one will be joining, though the reception of new members is clearly listed as part of the morning Order of Worship. We're wondering how to handle an embarrassing situation.

Then Byron says, "Oh . . . and I just learned that Jesus is in the hospital."

1. Toynbee, "Why and How I Work."

"Which hospital?"

"I think it's Star," he says.

"What's Star? I've never heard of it."

"Oh," says Byron, "it's a private wing of Christ Hospital for public figures concerned about their privacy."

"When was he admitted, and why? What's the diagnosis?

"I don't know; I just learned of it a moment ago from John (the custodian)."

"Well . . . what should we do? The congregation will be shocked, but we should announce it. We should remember Jesus in the Prayers of Church, don't you think?"

The idea of Jesus being in the hospital didn't strike me as that strange in the dream, but it did pose its own kind of curious scenario. I'd never imagined Jesus sick. I wonder if Jesus was ever in the hospital? There was something strangely comforting about the thought of Jesus in the hospital, one of the flock for whom we could pray.

Dreams, they say, are how the subconscious works on things the conscious mind dares not address. What if Jesus had died in the hospital?

Biblical scholars and theologians interpret the church's sacred writings (Holy Scripture) in light of the different genres of literature. They also differentiate between the Jesus of history (Jesus of Nazareth), and the Jesus of faith (the crucified-risen Christ of believers). In Christian scripture the two are welded together. The Jesus story is told by four gospels: Matthew, Mark, Luke, and John. A Gospel is, by its very nature, a witness to faith, written by faith to elicit faith in the reader, not an objective eye-witness account of events in the life of Jesus as a video camera might have given us. The only access we have to Jesus of Nazareth is through the eyes of faith in Jesus as the Christ.

The theological tradition of the church has always insisted on the full humanity of Jesus. His humanity was only half the Chalcedonian Formula (fully divine, fully human), but Jesus's humanity is the starting place for any claim to the Formula's other half: the divinity of Jesus Christ. Time after time there have arisen fanciful representations of Jesus. In some of these, the historical Jesus is obliterated. He wears flesh and blood the way an actor playing a part on stage assumes a costume to draw the audience into the play. In these versions of Christian faith, the bodily Jesus is a disguise for God.

But a Jesus who was never sick a day in his life, a Jesus without bodily functions, pains, and hungers, a Jesus who didn't feel the hammer slam his thumb at his carpenter's bench, a Jesus who couldn't be admitted to the emergency room in need of a transfusion, is not one of us. That Jesus is a figment of imagination.

Why I dreamed of Jesus in the hospital remains a mystery. What I know is that the dream wouldn't have come without a deep sense of Jesus, the Jesus of history and the Jesus of faith.

James Gustafson expressed the sentiment and sense of it after years of thoughtful reflection on the Christian faith. "The only good reason for claiming to be Christian," he wrote, "is that we continue to be empowered, sustained, renewed, informed, and judged by Jesus' incarnation of theocentric piety and fidelity."[2]

Jesus pointed beyond himself. He bowed his head to the Holy One who was greater than he. In his life he incarnated a God-centered faith and moral responsibility. The only way I know to love Jesus is to love those who could end up in the hospital or hospice care. They are Jesus. Jesus is us.

2. Gustafson, *Ethics*, 277.

When the Breath Flies Away

But what was before us we know not,
And we know not what shall succeed.
Haply, the river of Time—
As it grows, as the towns on its marge
Fling their wavering lights
On a wider, statelier stream—
May acquire, if not the calm
Of its early mountainous shore,
Yet a solemn peace of its own.

And the width of the waters, the hush
Of the grey expanse where he floats,
Freshening its current and spotted with foam
As it draws to the Ocean, may strike
Peace to the soul of the man on its breast—
As the pale waste widens around him,
As the banks fade dimmer away,
As the stars come out, and the night-wind
Brings up the stream
Murmurs and scents of the infinite sea.

—Matthew Arnold[1]

1. Arnold, "The Future," in *Empedocles on Etna*, 69–87.

When the Breath Flies Away

It takes only a moment to see oneself in the experience of Andy Catlett in Wendell Berry's story, "Fly Away, Breath!"[2] Our experience is of time flown away and flying away.

> Most of us, most of the time, think mostly of the past. Even when we say, "We are living now," we can only mean that we were living a moment ago.
>
> Nevertheless, in this sometimes horrifying, sometimes satisfying, never sufficiently noticed present, between a past mostly forgotten and a future that we deserve to fear but cannot predict, some few things can be recalled.

We are creatures of a specific time and place and relationships: with loved ones, friends, and enemies; with a plot of land, a town or city we call home; with a state, a nation, a world in time sandwiched between past and future that we call the present.

A ghost town is a reminder of time. Southern Cross stands on the mountain high above Georgetown Lake, Montana, where the vistas are breathtaking, and the past is barely remembered except for the abandoned miners' quarters and mine shafts below the surface of the place that remind the visitor of the fickleness of time.

"All flesh is grass" and yet, despite our intuitive awareness of it, we unconsciously pretend most days that it is untrue that "the grass withers, the flower fades" (Isa 40:8).

"Nevertheless," says Wendell Berry, "between a past mostly forgotten and a future that we deserve to fear but cannot predict, some few things can be recalled"—things like my friendship with Phil, now ended unexpectedly by a rare, nearly impossible to diagnose lymphoma in his spleen. Hours before his death, the interventionist ICU doctor described Phil's case and his ten days in the ICU as "a real shit storm" because of the many ongoing complications that mystified the medical staff. In all of medical history, only ten to fifteen cases have been reported where lymphoma originated in the spleen. By the time it was discovered in Phil, other organs had begun to shut down. The first organ to go

2. Berry, "Fly Away, Breath (1907)," in *A Place in Time*, 15.

was the gallbladder, which was already abscessed when they operated to remove the spleen.

Medical professionals are no different from the rest of us, except for their skill and training in how to treat illness and preserve life. Despite every effort to keep the present from slipping into the past, against every attempt to retain some kind of future, the breath always flies away.

Phil's death, as I had come to see it days before he passed, came as an act of mercy, a release from the torturous interventions of advanced medical technology that asks the question, "How?" without first asking, "Why?"

I'm increasingly convinced that the denial of death (mortality) and the search for immortality are the opposites of the Christian faith in God—in Hebrew YHWH ("I am Who I Am / I will Be Who I will be")—who alone is eternal. All else is species hubris, the refusal to live thankfully, graciously, and peacefully within the limits of finite, mortal goodness.

We are all standing in line, not knowing at what time or place our time will come. We're all headed for the ghost town, thinking of the past or dreading the future we deserve, but also, in moments of grace, remembering with thanksgiving the tender mercies along the way that cannot be denied.

I do not know what of Phil or any of us may lie beyond the grave, an odd thing to say for a minister of the gospel whose faith lives out of the life, death, and resurrection of Jesus. Knowing my unknowing, my best friend echoed Jesus's question to Nicodemus about the not entirely unrelated matter of being born of the Spirit: "You are the teacher of God's people and don't know these things?"

I confess to knowing very little, especially when what Chaim Potok calls the four-o'clock-in-the-morning questions wake me in the middle of the night between a present now gone and a future that remains inscrutable. However that may be, what I do know is that bodily life—mortal life in space and time in the midst of eternity—is what we have, and it is to be cherished. Bound to the limits of time and place, it is God's good creation. Yet only God is the Eternal One.

Whatever lies on the other side of my years is beyond my mortal knowing. But I can and do affirm the eternity of God and the scriptural point of view that whether we live or whether we die, we belong to the Lord. "All flesh is grass. The grass withers, the flower fades, but the Word of our God (YHWH, the eternal) shall last forever." Right now, in good conscience, that's enough bread to live on today as I recall the blessing of Phil and pray for all who loved him.

The Forlorn Children of the *Mayflower*

We go back to the *Mayflower*,
but to a murderer found there.
No property or position,
No wealth, no fame, or profession.
No beauties seen now or then,
but we managed to have children.

—Steve Shoemaker[1]

Uncle John claimed we Andrews descended from John Alden and Priscilla Mullins of the *Mayflower*. He spent many years, day after day, doing the research to confirm what every Yankee wants to find: a connection that makes them "blue bloods," descendants of the English settlers who arrived at Plymouth Rock on the *Mayflower*.

I always wondered, though, why such an important family as John Alden's and Priscilla Mullins's would live in South Paris, Maine. Had Mark Twain known about the place, he would have said of it what he wrote about Cincinnati: "When the end of the world comes, I want to be in Cincinnati. It's always ten years

1. Shoemaker, "Our Family Bush."

behind the times." I've lived in Cincinnati. I've also lived in South Paris. South Paris wins the contest hands down.

Thinking of South Paris, a feeling sweeps over me. A kind of despair. I feel forlorn.

I went back to South Paris for Aunt Gertrude's memorial service. As always, I wondered why people chose to live there. My cousins grew up there in Oxford County, the poorest county in the state of Maine. Most of them couldn't wait to leave and did as soon as they could and never looked back. I wondered why the others stayed. But even more, I've wondered why our forebears went there at all, being especially important blue bloods like the family of John Alden and Priscilla Mullins of the *Mayflower*.

The Andrews family didn't start out in South Paris, though. They settled a few miles away, before South Paris existed, in the pristine foothills of the White Mountains on wooded land with a trout stream over which they would build a red covered bridge and a paddlewheel sawmill to mill the lumber for things like caskets. The Andrews Casket Company and Funeral Home became a staple of the hamlet, the famed institution of an entrepreneurial Baptist minister, John Alden's descendant, Isaac Andrews. The property remained in the family for over two hundred years until several years ago my mother's favorite cousin, Lynwood ("Pete") Andrews, sold his home, the casket company, and the funeral home, along with the land to some whippersnapper.

A smile always came across my mother's face whenever she told us of playing hide-and-seek with her siblings, Gertrude, John, Elwood, and Roy in the casket room of the original Andrews homestead in Woodstock. Imagine hiding in a casket. Maybe everyone in those woods had come there to hide from death, running from the haunted memory of the murders that followed their landing at Plymouth Rock where they once had "no property or position, no wealth, no fame, or profession, no beauties seen now or then, but . . . managed to have children."

In my childhood, my mother and I often visited Grandpa Andrews, my great grandfather, who still lived on the original Andrews property with the casket factory, the trout stream, the red covered bridge, the mill, the funeral home, and the family home. By the time I came along, he was infirm, cared for by his live-in housekeeper. Angie was a sweet woman who dearly loved Grandpa Andrews. Angie made the best buttermilk biscuits anyone had ever tasted; no one could duplicate them, even with the recipe she shared. My mother always suspected there was a secret ingredient missing from the public recipe. There was a wink-wink when anyone spoke of Angie as the housekeeper. She was known for her biscuits. The rest was nobody's business.

I was three and four years old when my mother and I lived in South Paris and made the visits to Grandpa Andrews. It was during the Second World War. My father was overseas in the South Pacific. Even then, I sensed the smell of death, knowing in my bones that one of the caskets in the casket room might be waiting for my father. Even way back then, I could smell the forlornness in the air.

On a Sunday two days before doing Aunt Gertrude's service, I was on my way to the Mollyockett Inn near the old Andrews homestead in Woodstock when, a mile or so before my destination, a sign advertising whole-bellied fried clams caught my eye. I love fried clams. We don't get those in Minnesota. I pulled into the parking lot. A man whose home shared the driveway to the little restaurant was standing outside.

"Can I help ya?" he asked.

"Well, I don't know. I saw the sign for fried clams," I said, "but it looks like it's closed."

"Well, it's Sunday," he said. "Where ya from?"

"Minnesota. We don't get whole-bellied fried clams in Minnesota."

"Wait right here," he said. "We'll open up. Let me go in and get the missus."

Inside the restaurant, he asked where I'm from and what brings me to these parts. "I'm here for a funeral. I'm staying at the Mollyockett," I said.

"You must be here for Pete's funeral."

"Pete? Pete who?"

"Well, Pete Andrews."

"Pete died? No, I'm here for my aunt Gertrude's service. She was Pete's first cousin, and my mother's favorite cousin. Pete died?"

"Well, golly!" he said. "I thought it was a little early. He just died yesterday, wasn't it, Mabel? It was. It was yesterday, Saturday, right, Mabel? I thought you was here for Pete's funeral.

"See that dollar bill up there?" he said, pointing to a framed dollar bill behind the lunch counter. "That's from Pete. Our first customer. We'd just moved here from Rhode Island. Real gentleman, that Pete. Always had a different lady with him, a real ladies' man, but always a gentleman. Always wore a white shirt and tie."

I wonder if Pete carried the forlornness of the children of the *Mayflower*, running from a murderous ancestral history he couldn't identify, trying to resolve it while playing among the caskets, or eating fried clams with the ladies. Always the gentleman, just like Isaac Andrews, his grandfather, and all the other blue-blooded Aldens before him. Forlorn and wondering why.

Forlornness is part of the Andrews DNA. As children of the *Mayflower*, we carry the blues, but we can't put our finger on their source. We are the people of racial, religious, and national exceptionalisms gone bad. Unlike America's slaughtered indigenous people and those who came as slaves on "the Good Ship Jesus,"[2] we have not been taught to sing our blues. We are not privileged to carry the legacy of the blues as Otis Moss III describes it:

> The Blues is a cultural legacy that dares to see the American landscape from the viewpoint of the underside. Ralph Ellison, the literary maven and cultural critic, states, "The blues is an impulse to keep the painful details and episodes of a brutal experience alive in one's aching consciousness."[3]

Our black and red sisters' and brothers' aching consciousness is the trans-generational pain of victimization—massacres, the

2. "Good Ship Jesus" was the nickname of the first slave ship to deliver its "cargo" of captured Africans to the Americas. The logo on its front was two Africans bound back to back.

3. Moss, *Blue Note Preaching*, 5.

hold of a slave ship, and the lynching tree. The aching consciousness of the white children of the *Mayflower* is different, but no less blue—the transgenerational, subliminal consciousness of the dashed illusions of racial and religious exceptionalism that did the victimizing.

If Otis Moss's *Blue Note* offers a balm in Gilead to heal the wounded souls of those who have lived on America's "underside," it also offers the balm "that heals the *sin-sick* soul"[4] of the murderers—the ashen gray, amnesiac, forlorn souls haunted by the shadow of the systemic guilt of white privilege, religious exceptionalism, and national manifest destiny, yet still bowing at the altar of the old system: nationalistic, imperialistic capitalism.

4. Though there is no consensus regarding the origins of "A Balm in Gilead," it is thought to depend, in part, on John Newton's hymn "The Good Physician." Newton turned around his slave ship and wrote "Amazing Grace."

The Stories We Tell Ourselves

People are trapped in history
and history is trapped inside of them.

—James Baldwin[1]

For black and red peoples in North America,
the spirit of the Enlightenment was socially
and politically demonic, becoming a pseudo-intellectual
basis for their enslavement or extermination.

—James H. Cone[2]

A month in America's oldest city, St. Augustine, Florida, makes clear that history is a strange thing. History is the past, but it's also the telling of it, the renderings of it. The English language does not distinguish between the two—the past as it was, and the past as remembered and interpreted. Only the interpreted past is available to us.

Historians distinguish between the two with the word 'history' (the past) and 'historiography', defined by the *Oxford English*

1. Baldwin, *Notes of a Native Son*, 168.
2. Cone, *God of the Oppressed*, 46.

Dictionary as "the study of historical writings or the writing of history."

Most interesting during our one-month stay in St. Augustine were the different historiographies of the civil rights movement.

Tourists in St. Augustine walk past homes and churches with plaques like this one that tell the story of the brave civil rights history of the '50s and '60s on what's called the Freedom Trail. The casual tourist is unlikely to notice that the Freedom Trail story is not the only one in town. There are two different sets of plaques. The groups that wrote and erected them represent different, often competing historiographies.

The more prominent set of plaques that define the Freedom Trail were created by ACCORD.[3] They highlight the role of the Reverend Dr. Martin Luther King Jr. and the Southern Christian Leadership Conference (SCLC).

The other is the project of a group of local citizens led by the Eubanks family, whose father, the Reverend Goldie M. Eubanks Sr., was vice president of the St. Augustine chapter of the National Association for the Advancement of Colored People (NAACP), whose work predated and continued after the arrival of Dr. King and the SCLC in St. Augustine.

The NAACP is the oldest civil rights organization in America. In the 1950s and '60s, many civil rights leaders came to regard it as too passive, too conservative. The word "colored" in its name labeled it as out of touch with black pride. The Reverend Dr. Martin Luther King Jr. and the SCLC arose as a bolder, more active organization, although the SCLC and the NAACP, represented by Dr. King and Roy Wilkins respectively, worked closely together. To the left of the SCLC, the Student Nonviolent Coordinating Committee (SNCC) and the Congress of Racial Equality (CORE) joined them on the national stage.

3. ACCORD is the acronym for the Anniversary to Commemorate the Civil Rights Demonstrations, established in 2004 to celebrate the fortieth anniversary of the Civil Rights Act of 1964. Its mission is "remembering, recognizing, and honoring all those who risked their lives to attain civil rights for all and celebrating St. Augustine's pivotal role in the Civil Right Act of 1964."

While in St. Augustine, we lived next door to a home on the Freedom Trail identified by ACCORD as important to the movement in St. Augustine. Some of the men who gathered there every midmorning until dark seem to identify with Dr. King and the SCLC. Others seem resentful that Dr. King and the SCLC got the praise for the work of Rev. Eubanks, Rev. Thomas, and Dr. Robert Hayling, a courageous local dentist who paved the way for national media attention to the plight in St. Augustine. The historiography of the latter group is posted on the alternative plaques that focus more on the indigenous leaders who put their lives on the line every day as citizens of St. Augustine.

History and historiography are like that. The four gospels of the New Testament look at the same time period and events with different memories and different angles on the Jesus story. The nature of history is that it always leaves itself to interpretation. And the nature of historiography is that it raises the question of the storyteller's angle.

In light of Dr. King's later speeches about the intrinsic connection between capitalism, the war in Vietnam, and militarism, it seems a great paradox that it was the Northrop Grumman Corporation, one of the largest Department of Defense contractors, that funded the ACCORD project centered on Dr. King. History and historiography are always strange. Always they involve some concoction of our better selves, self-interest, pride, and sometimes, a heavy dose of irony.

The Man Who Knew

A convictional world view is "a being-related-to" the world which involves a person's existential center. . . . It is connected with the deepest layers of our personality, i.e., to what we really are.

—Willem Zuurdeeg[1]

He knows who he is! He is not ignorant; he's smart. He knows the visiting rabbi is both "the Holy One of God" and the one who has "come to destroy us."

It is because he knows this that he is shrieking from the back row. He knows better than those around him, all the others who have come at sundown to observe Shabbat.

He takes his customary place among his neighbors in the Capernaum synagogue. He does not expect much to happen. Everyone, including him, knows he's a little strange. Off balance, as the kinder of them say. Not the norm. Both they and he know his place. None of them yet knows Annie Dillard's advice that worshipers "should wear crash helmets. Ushers should issue life preservers and signal flares; they should lash us to our pews. For the

1. Zuurdeeg, *Man Before Chaos*, 25.

sleeping god may wake some day and take offense, or the waking god may draw us out to where we can never return."[2]

They have no need for crash helmets, life preservers, or signal flares. The mad man is like the ones who are better balanced: he likes his safety. He is safe in his customary place among the customary people expecting a customary teaching from a customary teacher who teaches like a parrot (a scribe). He expects to leave the same way he has come: bored and boring in the daily-ness of it all.

They look at him. He looks at them. They all yawn. Until the guest rabbi takes his seat to teach and says nothing. Jesus just looks over the congregation, reading their faces, reading their minds, looking into their hearts. They become uncomfortable with the long silence. He is reading them like a book he's read too many times.

When finally the rabbi speaks, he astounds them. He reads the Torah and the prophets as living texts, not history. He is alive and expectant. He is not bored or boring. He teaches with authority. He commands the attention of the room. They want him, but do not want him. They haven't brought crash helmets. They've come for safety—their weekly fix of the "protect-from-danger religion" and the "happy-ending religion" that has displaced Moses and the prophets.

He catches the eye of the man who's a little off balance, whose frequent uninvited outbursts long ago placed him in the back row of the assigned seating. Although the rabbi's eyes are working the room from left to right and back again, seeing all the faces there, it is as though he is staring at him alone. They are all a bit on edge now, drawn to the rabbi's voice and the content of his teaching, his unparalleled authority, but they are also becoming nervous that he is challenging the convictional world that keeps them from who and what they really are as the children of Abraham and Sarah.

The man in the back senses this. He knows this. He begins to twitch and make strange sounds. He is agitated, disturbed, out of his comfort zone like everyone else. His face twitching with the familiar tic, he struggles to his feet from his back row seat, shoving

2. Dillard, *Teaching a Stone to Talk*, 40–41.

from his shoulders the hands of the ushers stationed on either side of him to prevent the man with Tourette Syndrome from disturbing them and making a fool of himself.

He points at the rabbi and shrieks at him: "What have you to do with us, Jesus of Nazareth? Have you come to destroy us? I know who you are, the Holy One of God."

Jesus moves from the center to the back row. He tells the bodyguards to leave him alone. He stands eye to eye with him. "Be silent," he says, as though speaking not to the man himself but to others who torment him from the inside. "Come out of him."

The whole congregation is on their feet watching. They know that the Tourette man with the tic and uncontrollable speech has spoken for all of the normal ones as well. "Have you come to destroy us?"

The man screams and convulses, but it is not the man who is convulsing; it is the hostage-takers whose powers are being broken who are convulsing: the fear of losing one's assigned place, the customary despair and despairing comfort that robs him and all of them of the joy of the extraordinary in ordinary life.

Perhaps the story of "the man with the evil spirit" (Mark 1:21–28) comes so early in the Gospel of Mark because it is the story of us all. The Holy One of God does come to destroy us as well as heal us. The next time you go to the synagogue for Sabbath rest or to church on a Sunday morning, take a crash helmet and expect something great to happen!

The Church on the Bridge

Have we not come to such
an impasse in the modern world
that we must love our enemies—or else?

—Martin Luther King Jr.

If some churches are like opium dens, others are like Pettus Bridge, the bridge over the Alabama River you must cross to get from Selma to Montgomery, Alabama.

In the history of America's civil rights movement, Pettus Bridge and the events of Bloody Saturday represent a crossing over from the society addicted to violence, hatred, and war to "the peaceable kingdom" of Isaiah. Think Jesus. Think Martin Luther King Jr. Think Congressman John Lewis. Think all the anonymous, courageous souls who dared to cross the bridge from here to there.

"Have we not come to such an impasse in the modern world that we must love our enemies—or else?" asked Dr. King. "The chain reaction of evil—hate begetting hate, wars producing more wars—must be broken, or else we shall be plunged into the dark abyss of annihilation."[1]

I suspect Karl Marx never knew a church like that. What he saw was religion as a tool of the powerful, an ideological overlay

1. King, *Strength to Love*, 53.

on reality to keep their subjects compliant with the existing social order.

The church on the bridge is no opium den. No one is doped up. No one is in a stupor. People don't go there to hide. It is by nature a place that calls for commitment and action. The church as Pettus Bridge is spiritually, economically, politically, and culturally revolutionary. It requires far-reaching transformation of people, structures, and systems. It's a risky place. The church on the bridge requires you to put your whole body, mind, and soul on the line—on the bridge—fully conscious that the troops of the old social order will come after you. It is the church of Jesus and the prophets, and of Paul at his best:

> I appeal to you therefore, brothers and sisters, by the mercies of God, to present your bodies as a living sacrifice, holy and acceptable to God, which is your spiritual worship. Do not be conformed to this world, but be transformed by the renewing of your minds, so that you may discern what is the will of God—what is good and acceptable and perfect. (Rom 12:1–2)

Every time the Church on the Bridge gathers for worship, the pews are filled with people wearing crash helmets. They expect something real to happen. They expect to make it happen. When they gather around the Lord's Table for Eucharist, they know what they are celebrating: "the peaceable kingdom," the city of God on the other side of the violence, hatred, and war that put them on the bridge.

Martin Luther King Day in St. Augustine

Forgetfulness transforms every occurrence
into a nonoccurrence.

—Plutarch

The car dealer here in St. Augustine will be open on Martin Luther King Jr. Day. No holiday for its workers.

I learn this while waiting for my car to be serviced. I read the local paper, *The St. Augustine Record*, Wednesday, January 14, 2015. Tucked away on page A6 under "News and Notes" is a small headline: "Commemorative Breakfast Planned."

Commemorative of what? Martin Luther King Jr., Monday, January 19, at First Coastal Technical College.

I put down the paper and walk through the show room to look at the new models. A white sales manager sees me get into one of the cars and points angrily to a twenty-something African-American salesman to get with the program. The young man greets me through the passenger window. I tell him I'm just killing time during a routine oil change and that I'm from Minnesota. We exchange pleasantries.

I get a cup of coffee and go out to look at the used cars—it's my thing, checking out used cars—and run into the young salesman again. I ask whether Martin Luther King Jr. Day is a big deal here in St. Augustine. He smiles. I tell him I've just read the newspaper and the small announcement.

"Is the dealership closed for Martin Luther King Jr. Day?" I ask.

"No, sir. We're open," he says. "I'll be working."

"Do you know about the St. Augustine Four?" I ask. He doesn't. I tell him we're staying next door to the home of James and Hattie White, whose fourteen-year-old son Samuel was sent to reform school in 1963 for sitting in at the Woolworth's lunch counter and that the case of the four teenagers was responsible for Dr. King and Jackie Robinson joining the cause in St. Augustine.

Before I leave the dealership, he finds me in the waiting area. "I asked the boss," he says. "He said I can have the day off if I want it."

I tell him there's a "Hands Up!" workshop Saturday morning at the St. Paul African Methodist Episcopal Church (AME) where MLK and Jackie Robinson joined the local civil rights movement in St. Augustine. It's just around the corner from where we're staying in Lincolnville.

"Come if you can!"

"Thanks," he says, "Maybe I'll see you there."

The Neighbors in St. Augustine

> Race is the most explosive issue in American life precisely because it forces us to confront the tragic facts of poverty and paranoia, despair and distrust. In short, a candid examination of *race* matters takes us to the core of the crisis of American democracy.
>
> —Cornel West[1]

The men gather late in front of the house every morning before the resident gets up.

Mostly in their sixties and early seventies, they arrive on bicycles or on foot with paper bags scrunched close at the top. The minority, the younger ones in their twenties, don't use bags. They don't hide the beer can or the pint. They pull the cheap, green, plastic chairs from the yard out to the sidewalk to start the day.

The older ones survived the St. Augustine civil rights movement of the early '60s and the violent reaction of the white city fathers to the passage of the Civil Rights Act. They tell stories. The younger men don't seem to care.

I walk next door most every day to say hello. The conversations become windows into humanity, disparate perspectives, and history itself.

1. West, *Race Matters*, 107.

Why did the once young men who waded in at Butler Beach in 1964, survived the firebombing of their homes and the beatings by the Ku Klux Klan, end up here bleary-eyed with paper bags?

They grow louder as the day wears on. One of them stands in the middle of the street blocking traffic as if to say to passersby, "This is OUR neighborhood!" Several times a day a car pulls up to the curb, opens the window, and exchanges something with the men. They disappear, one by one, into the house for a time.

At noon one day I walk next door and find myself in the middle of what appears to be an argument between one of the older men sitting in the yard and a twenty-something man sitting on the sidewalk with his back turned to the street. I come by to say hello. The older man greets me. We say good morning.

"You're a reverend, right?"

"Well, yes. Sort of"—I smile—"more or less reverent." We enjoy a good laugh.

"So," he says, pointing to the young man holding his open Pabst Blue Ribbon, "doesn't the Bible say, 'Instead of giving a man a fish, you should teach him how to fish?'"

"Well, no. The Bible doesn't say that, but it's pretty close to some of what the Bible teaches."

"See," says the young man, "I told you the Bible doesn't say that!"

The civil rights movement survivors recall how some of their classmates got out of town and left them behind. One of them owns upscale hotels in Atlanta and Miami. He comes home in his big Mercedes every five years or so. According to the men next door, he and others who got out look down their noses at the shrimp boat workers who live hand-to-mouth existences in the old neighborhood where they grew up together.

The civil rights movement in St. Augustine is still a matter of debate both among its veterans and among the young men who have no living memory of it. For young and old alike, the men who gather daily next door are a community to each other. They have taken their "place" in the post–civil rights movement era of St. Augustine.

They are part of America's left behind. They're going nowhere their feet or bicycles can't take them. They care about each other. They are without pretense. They have each other, old friends and younger ones who are going nowhere. They are a local chapter of the community of the stuck. Their numbers are growing all across America.

Hands Up! Don't Carve!

"I hope I don't get killed
for being black today."[1]

A decade before Black Lives Matter captured the news, a nineteen-year-old African-American man insists on seeing the Legal Rights Center's executive director.[2]

He's a large man, his speech is fast, his eyes are angry. He pulls up his shirt to show the swastika he alleges the police of the Fourth Precinct carved on his back with a key after pushing him face down on the pavement in North Minneapolis.[3]

There are witnesses. Three women and a man sitting on a front porch saw it happen. Raymond, we'll call him, was objecting to the arrest of another man when two officers forced Raymond down to the pavement, face down, while one of the officers used his key to etch the swastika into his flesh. Raymond was not arrested. The incident is not on the police log.

1. This statement by a Black Lives Matter movement protester has come to symbolize the community's view of the police and police practices.

2. Legal Rights Center (LRC) is a nonprofit public defense corporation. "A law firm of and for the people," founded by African-American and American Indian civil rights movements in 1970. http://www.legalrightscenter.org/.

3. Minneapolis's predominantly African-American north side is the poorest section of the city where the Minneapolis Police Department's pattern of excessive force is etched into the consciousness of residents.

Police abuse of power, racial profiling, the use of unreasonable force, shootings, and prosecutors and grand juries looking the other way always have been the way it is in America. What's new is the public outcry, the jarring of consciousness and conscience among those who do not live in places like North Minneapolis, or the poorer neighborhoods of Ferguson, Baltimore, Cleveland, or New York City.

After several years of referring complainants to the Minneapolis Police Civilian Review Board without satisfaction or remedy, I proposed something out of the ordinary. With Raymond's agreement, we went directly to the commanding officer of the Minneapolis Police Department's Fourth Precinct.

Sitting behind his desk, the commander seemed preoccupied with paperwork. That changed when Raymond pulled up his shirt to reveal the swastika. The commander asked if Raymond got the number of the squad car or remembered the badge numbers or names of the officers. He didn't. Then, to our great surprise, he did something altogether unexpected. He asked Raymond whether he remembered the first initial of either of the officers. "Like, did the names begin with a 'B' or a 'C'?" An officer whose name begins with 'B' is well known for terrorizing the North Minneapolis African-American community. His nickname on the street begins with a 'B': "Butcher."

"This is way beyond Internal Investigation," he said. "You need to take this to the FBI."

Raymond didn't trust the FBI any more than he trusted the Minneapolis Police Department. He decided to let it go.

Lots of people like Raymond have decided over the years to let it go. Until Michael Brown was shot and killed in Ferguson and a grand jury decided not to indict the officer. Until twelve-year-old Tamir Rice was killed by a police officer in Cleveland. Until Eric Garner died of a police officer's chokehold saying, "I can't breathe!" The inferno of anger boiling over across the streets of America is new only in the breadth of consciousness and conscience.

It will take time. It will take a change of heart and mind. But, mostly, it will not change until America gets it straight that, for most African-Americans, being black is also an issue of class. Class is about power and powerlessness. Only when what we call "the middle class" understands that its interests lie with people in neighborhoods like North Minneapolis, Ferguson, Cleveland, Baltimore, and New York City will black lives matter in America.

It's all about the economics: up or down. There really is no middle.

"Don't carve!"

"I can't breathe!"

Homeland Militarization

It has lately come to pass that America has entered upon a dark age. . . . It is, I believe, an authentic dark age; that is, a time in which the power of death is pervasive and militant, and in which people exist without hope.

—William Stringfellow[1]

The helicopters that had been sent to Iraq and Afghanistan to protect us here at home were flying around downtown Minneapolis and St. Paul. The Blackhawk helicopters were on "urban training exercises," rattling the windows of residents' condos, homes, and apartments right here at home in Minnesota.[2]

Why were they here? When did a city of civilians become the training grounds for the US Army, and why has there not been a louder outcry against the intrusive presence of the military into what we have now come to call "the homeland"? Perhaps because we believe it makes us safer, but citizen preoccupation with security is the spawning ground for national security states.

1. Stringfellow, *An Ethic for Christians*, 13. William Stringfellow was a constitutional lawyer and lay theologian whose persistent theme was the "Constantinian compromise"—the subsuming of Christianity to the interests of empire. During a visit to the United States, Karl Barth advised Americans to listen to Stringfellow.

2. Duchschere, "Return of Blackhawk Copters."

A day after the Pew Research Center issued its report on the strikingly divergent attitudes of whites and blacks about law enforcement following the death of Michael Brown, US Attorney General Eric Holder went to Missouri to meet with leaders there. According to the Pew Center,

> [B]lacks and whites have sharply different reactions to the police shooting of an unarmed teen in Ferguson, Missouri, and the protests and violence that followed. Blacks are about twice as likely as whites to say that the shooting of Michael Brown "raises important issues about race that need to be discussed." Wide racial differences also are evident in opinions about whether local police went too far in the aftermath of Brown's death, and in confidence in the investigations into the shooting.[3]

A LASTING MEMORY

I live in a predominantly white middle-class community southwest of downtown Minneapolis. The police aren't around much except to pick up a dead opossum that tried to cross the state highway. We don't think much about the police where I live. But I also have a memory from the summer of 1968 that puts me with those who believe that race and institutional violence—particularly police violence—are tied together in places like Ferguson and North Minneapolis and other places that feel to their residents like a military occupation.

The time I'm remembering came on the heels of The National Commission on Civil Disorders, known as the Kerner Commission,[4] which warned that "our nation is moving toward two societies, one black, one white—separate and unequal." Presi-

3. Pew Research Center, "Stark Racial Divisions."

4. The National Advisory Commission on Civil Disorders was an eleven-member commission established by President Lyndon B. Johnson to investigate the causes of the 1967 race riots in the United States and to provide recommendations for the future. It was referred to as the Kerner Commission after its chair, Governor Otto Kerner Jr. of Illinois.

dent Lyndon B. Johnson rejected the commission's multiple recommendations for addressing the problem of growing economic disparity between whites and blacks.

Back then I was a twenty-six-year-old assistant pastor at a downtown church in Decatur, Illinois. What I experienced in the church parking lot etched the report's findings in my heart and mind. I've never seen our society the same since.

The summer program for youth from the public housing projects let out at ten o'clock at night. Ninety-eight percent of the kids in Teen Town were black. The program had been a success by every measure, drawing one hundred to five hundred youth from the tenements to the downtown church on any given night. Until a neighbor from the apartment building next to the church called the police at closing time.

By the time I made it up the stairs from the recreation room, the squad cars were plunging into the crowd, billy clubs swinging in every direction, mace being sprayed indiscriminately in the kids' faces, police officers choking the program's assistant director with a billy club, handcuffing him and shoving him into the back of the paddy wagon.

That night, forty store windows were broken in downtown Decatur near the church. I drove home, slapped on my clerical collar and waded into the melee. It was clear to me that this was what the Kerner Commission described. This was the result of a police riot. It should never have happened.

Neither should it have happened in Ferguson, Missouri. You don't need to shoot a kid six times—and the sight of law-enforcement officers riding armored tanks with guns pointed at civilians reignites the enduring embers of the tragedy of race in America.

BLURRING THE LINE BETWEEN MILITARY AND CIVILIAN LIFE

The Kerner Commission Report was issued as a result of urban civil disturbances in America's major cities. It spoke of race and police and National Guard violence—a systemic problem that threatened American society itself. Back then armored tanks with gun turrets patrolled the streets of Detroit. This month the very same thing happened with one important difference: this time, those who patrolled the streets were dressed in camouflage pants that looked like US Marine or Army attire. That was in Ferguson, Missouri.

The Night Hawks in their Blackhawk helicopters flew around the Twin Cities from Monday through Thursday night. It is no assurance that, according to the unit's Fort Campbell, Kentucky, commander, the same "urban training exercises" had taken place in San Diego, Phoenix, and other major cities. It doesn't make it right. It provides little comfort to those who value keeping a hard line between military and civilian life.

Our military adventures abroad can have disastrous domestic consequences. What we sent off to Iraq and Afghanistan are now training in our backyards. The message the commander wants us to hear is that they are here to protect us, our best friends, as it were, among our neighbors. "There are terrorists in every city," he said, wanting to assure us. But the presence of the "urban training" exercise feels more like an occupation by a national security state.

Ferguson, Missouri, and the Twin Cities of Minnesota are not in Iraq or Afghanistan, but they feel more and more like they are every day.

The questions are moral and spiritual, just as they were when the Kerner Commission identified the drift toward two societies: one white, one black. Just as they were in Abu Ghraib. Just as they are now when the US Army special forces unit is using our own cities as military training grounds . . . for what purpose?

HOW DO WE STOP THIS BEFORE WE'RE ALL DEAD OPOSSUMS?

Constitutional lawyer, civil rights attorney, and theologian William Stringfellow offered a strange wake-up call to American citizens who might choose to roll over and play dead. Long before the downtown training exercise in Minneapolis, he wrote,

Homeland Militarization

My concern is to understand America biblically. The effort is to comprehend the nation, to grasp what is happening right now to the nation and to consider the destiny of the nation within the scope and style of the ethics and ethical metaphors distinctive to the biblical witness in history. The task is to treat the nation within the tradition of biblical politics, to understand America biblically—not the other way around, not (to put it in an appropriately awkward way) to construe the Bible Americanly.[5]

5. Stringfellow, *An Ethic for Christians*, 13.

Jacob Miller's Amish Rocking Chair

In a world where repaying evil with evil
is almost second nature, the Amish
remind us there's a better way.

—Sister Helen Prejean[1]

I am not Amish. I really like my car. I like the internet. I have an insurance policy. I like electricity. But I do have an Amish rocking chair. I bought the rocker from Jacob Miller, an Amish craftsman in Millersburg, Ohio. We sat on his front porch and rocked awhile. I paid him thirty dollars for the rocker made by Jacob's hands of maple and hickory. That was thirty years ago. In times like this, I still sit and rock. I think about Jacob and the Amish . . . but mostly, I'm thinking about the rest of us.

In the aftermath of the Nickel Mines Amish school massacre in Pennsylvania, the pictures of Amish horse-drawn buggies came into our living rooms. While those camera shots drew us closer to the strange world of Amish simplicity, those same camera shots were an invasion of Amish values. The Amish do not use cameras and do not allow themselves to be photographed—to do

1. In Kraybill, Nolt, and Weaver-Zercher, *Amish Grace*. Quote appears inside front jacket.

so, according to Amish values, would be to engage in vanity and pride, the opposites of humility and community. In none of the camera shots did you see an Amish person interviewed on film.

Rooted in the radical wing of the sixteenth century Protestant Reformation, the Amish live by their own norms. They are a peaceful community. They shun the culture of individualism, war, and greed on the basis of the teachings of Jesus, which they take at face value. "You have heard that it was said you shall love your neighbor and hate your enemies, but I say to you . . . love your enemies and pray for those who persecute you."

They also believe that the truth sets us free, and that the ends never justify the means.

As I sit in Jacob's rocking chair, I long for Amish truthfulness in an election campaign in which lies, distortion, and misrepresentation are used to assassinate the character of one's opponents. Winning is everything. Truth is lying by the roadside on the road to Washington. The Amish values of honesty, unvarnished truth, and, when the truth is violated, confession and forgiveness, are like a warm light in the cold dark night of the soul and nation.

It was this society of simple truth and nonviolence that bore such surprising witness to the power of forgiveness as, on their way to the funerals, the long line of horses clip-clopped past the home of the man who had killed their children in a one-room schoolhouse. They nodded their heads to the family members who had come out to their porch, also filled with grief because of what their son, their husband, their father had done. They had invited the widow of the killer to join them at the private funeral. And, days later, when the man who had killed their children also was buried, the horses clip-clopped the buggies of seventy-five of them to his funeral in support of his grieving family.

In times like these, I sometimes turn off the television and rock a while in Jacob Miller's Amish rocker. I sit back and give thanks for the hope of a more peaceful, humbler, and more honest way to be human.

The World in an Oyster

Fair ocean shell, the poet's art is weak
To utter all thy rich variety!
How thou does shame him when he tries to speak,
And tell his ear the rapture of his eye!
I cannot paint as very truth requires
The gold-green gleam that o'er thee breaks and roves,
Nor follow up with words thy flying fires
Where'er the startled rose-light wakes and moves.
Ah! why perplex with all thy countless hues
The single-hearted sonnet? Fair thee well!
I give thee up to some gay lyric muse,
As fitful as thyself, thy tale to tell:
The quick-spent sonnet cannot do thee right
Nor in one flash deliver all thy light.

—Charles Tennyson Turner (1808–1879)[1]

We're at a turning point. Turner's fair ocean shells were dying in the Gulf of Mexico in the wake of the explosion of *Deepwater Horizon*. The language used to describe the crisis and the attempt to correct it express the deeper view toward nature that underlies the problem: "BP engineers said Saturday that the

1. Turner, *Collected Sonnets*, 348.

'top kill' technique had failed and, after consultation with government officials, they had decided to move on to another strategy."[2]

The "spill" in the Gulf of Mexico from the uncontrolled blow out of the *Deepwater Horizon* well—the crisis we could not seem to "kill"—puts before us the symptoms and consequences of a more fundamental crisis than the black goo choking the life out of the Gulf. The uncontrolled "blow out" raises basic questions about how we think of ourselves and the order of nature.

Years ago a group of pastors spent four days with the Chesapeake Bay Foundation, whose mission is to protect and clean up the Chesapeake Bay. Our time there began with a day on the bay sailing on a skipjack, one of the few remaining motorless vessels used to harvest oysters by the tens and hundreds of bushels from oyster beds. The director of the Chesapeake Bay Foundation and a veteran waterman named Earl, who had worked the bay for fifty-four years, took us to school about the importance of the oysters to the bay's ecosystem.

According to the Chesapeake Bay Foundation, "bringing back the Bay's once vast network of filter feeders remains a daunting task . . . as each adult oyster can filter and clean up to 50 gallons of water per day—gobbling up algae, and removing dirt and nitrogen pollution."[3] Fifteen years before our visit, the oyster population filtered the equivalent of all the water in the Chesapeake Bay in three days' time.

By the time of our visit, the oyster population had shrunk to a fraction of what it used to be. The oysters were close to extinction; the bay's natural filtering system was in danger. "It's humans who have done this," said the old waterman, who'd learned his trade on the Gulf of Mexico in Louisiana. "The oysters will come back; I have to believe they'll come back."

Others were less hopeful. The Maryland Department of Natural Resources discussed the damage to the wetlands and the estuaries, the seedbeds of life. It had sounded the alarm for public

2. Kaufman and Krauss, "BP Prepares to Take New Tack."

3. Chesapeake Bay Foundation, "A New Day, a New Way for Oyster Restoration."

action to protect the birthplaces of all the seafood we eat, the places on which the whole chain of life depends.

Long after the pastors' visit, the news transfixed the American public on *Deepwater Horizon* in the Gulf of Mexico, where the attempted "top kill" was failing, the "spill" spreading in every direction—not only on the Gulf's surface, but below the surface.[4] Seeing the poisoned oysters in the hands of Louisiana watermen whose livelihood depends on clean Gulf waters, I think of Earl and his skipjack.

"It's humans who have done this."

But it's not *every* human who has done this violence to the Gulf. It was not the indigenous people of North America nor was it the Moken people[5] ("the sea gypsies") who, because they see themselves as part of nature, anticipated the 2004 Asian tsunami that caught the rest of the world by surprise. The blame lies with a specific form of humanity known as Western culture that sees the human species as exceptional to nature, the master of nature.

The language of a conquering culture is not the language of cooperation with nature. "And God said, '. . . fill the earth and subdue it; and have dominion over the fish of the sea and the birds of the air and over every creeping thing that creeps upon the earth'" (Gen 1:28)—a view that has led to violence against nature. We use the language of violence—a "top kill"—to describe the attempt to plug the man-made hole releasing oil from below the sea bed that is killing the oysters, fish, and waterfowl.

Insofar as interpreters of the book of Genesis have shaped this Western hubris, my Judeo-Christian tradition bears responsibility for this crisis. No matter how much we seek to reinterpret or sugarcoat the Genesis injunction to subdue and have dominion, the idea of species exceptionalism springs from the Bible itself.

It's depressing.

I sink into despair and confession. Silence. Deep doubt about the faith itself. Then I remember a prayer Earl called to my attention on the skipjack years ago, the prayer of St. Basil from the

4. Smithsonian National Museum of Natural History, "The Gulf Oil Spill."

5. Perez, "Survival Tactics of Indigenous People."

fourth century that offers a humbler, wiser understanding of ourselves—a view, like the Moken people's, that sees the whole world in an oyster:

> The Earth is the Lord's and the fullness thereof. O God, enlarge within us the sense of kinship with all living things, our brothers and sisters the animals to whom You have given the Earth as their home in common with us. We remember with shame that in the past we have exercised the high dominion of man with ruthless cruelty, so that the voice of the Earth, which should have gone up to You in song, has been a groan of travail. May we realize that they live not for us alone, but for themselves and for You, and that they have the sweetness of life.[6]

6. Jones, "Animals in the World."

My Soul Waits in Silence

St. Augustine Beach, Florida

For God alone my soul waits in silence,
for my hope is from him. I wait in silence.

—Psalm 62:5

I wait in silence.

Withdrawing from the noisy men next door in St. Augustine, I am like the hermit crab crawling into the borrowed snail shell on St. Augustine Beach on Anastasia Island.[1]

This is the beach brave souls dared to integrate in 1964, a place where there had been no place to hide, the public "whites only" beach where the hermit crabs refused to hide when the billy clubs swung to drive them from the segregated beach. There are no billy clubs on the beach today, but I can still hear the tumult in the post–civil rights movement world. The shouting hurts my ears.

1. The nonviolent "wade-ins" brought national media attention to the civil rights movement in St. Augustine, Florida. Local black and white residents were beaten in the wade-ins, and were joined by staff members of the Southern Christian Leadership Conference (SCLC), including Rev. C. T. Vivian, Rev. Fred Shuttlesworth, Dorothy Cotton, Al Lingo, Rev. LaVert Taylor, Benjamin Van Clarke, Golden Frinks, Rev. S. B. Wells, Dana Swan, Willie Bolden, and J. T. Johnson.

> How long will you assail a person, will you batter your victim, all of you, as you would a leaning wall, a tottering fence? (Ps 62:3)

The world is noisy. Loud. Cacophonous. Bellowing blasts, bewailing, and bedlam in Beirut, Baghdad, and Boston hurt my ears. Hoping to leave it, I come to the beach where the tides know nothing of the color of my skin, my income, my worries or fears.

> For God alone my soul waits in silence,
> for my hope is from him.
> He alone is my rock and my salvation,
> my fortress; I shall not be shaken.
> On God rests my deliverance and my honor;
> my mighty rock, my refuge is in God. (Ps 62:5–7)

At low tide I crawl inside the borrowed shell looking for a respite from the noonday heat—my deliverance, my refuge, my fortress. But, even here, the noise follows me.

The blasts, buzzes, and bellowing echo inside the shell. Silence eludes me. Even here, I am a poor man, a mere breath, walking among the vendors and hawkers, resentful, angry, beset, a man of low estate.

> Those of low estate are but a breath,
> those of high estate are a delusion;
> in the balances they go up;
> they are together lighter than a breath.
> Put no confidence in extortion,
> and set no vain hopes on robbery;
> if riches increase, do not set your heart on them. (Ps 62:9–10)

Here I am a breath away from the madness of high estates indulged on the upper side of the sand dune that separates the beach from the street.

I wait in silence.

I ponder the speed outside the hermit crab's temporary home—the abandoned snail shell, the speed that is itself an illusion, a flight of hubris washed away by the tides of time. I remember the race to nowhere, the myths of ownership, invulnerability, control, and superiority that race through the minds of low and high estates alike.

I hear the distant shouts and screams from the integration of St. Augustine Beach that still plunge the despondent men next door into the oblivion of cheap booze, dope, and, maybe, crack. But the longer I wait and listen, my heart grows strangely calmer. Quieter. More at peace.

I come into the deeper Silence of the Breath once heard by the psalmist.

> Once God has spoken;
> twice have I heard this:
> that power belongs to God,
> and steadfast love belongs to you, O Lord.
> For you repay to all
> according to their work. (Ps 62:11–12)

In the wordless silence I hear the Word I've come to the beach to hear:

> Be still, and know that I am God. (Ps 46:10)

Two Universities

Paris and Liberty

"Let's teach them [i.e., Muslims]
a lesson if they ever show up here,"
Falwell told thousands of students here
Dec. 4, with an unsubtle reference to
a pistol in his back pocket. Five days
later, he announced plans to let
qualified students store guns in
residence halls for the first time.

—Nick Anderson[1]

When the president who presides over "the largest Christian university in the world" in Lynchburg, Virginia urges every student to buy a gun and get a permit to carry a concealed weapon, for whatever reason, it seems both oxymoronic and moronic. It's neither Christian nor smart. It's not what people do in college. They buy books, not guns. It's not consistent with the traditions and standards of higher education. Scholars and presidents of real universities don't talk like that.

In the thirteenth century CE, a young Thomas Aquinas (1225–1274) enrolled as a student of Christian theology and

1. Anderson, "For Many at Liberty University."

philosophy at one of the world's first universities, the University of Paris. His professors introduced him to the writings of Aristotle, Plato, and Maimonides in their original Greek and Latin languages, and to the Christian scriptures.

Lynchburg, Virginia, in the twenty-first century is a long way from Paris in the thirteenth century, and that's too bad for all of us in America where what Aquinas later called "willful ignorance" has become the order of the day.

Thomas Aquinas wrote,

> It is clear that not every kind of ignorance is the cause of a sin, but that alone which removes the knowledge which would prevent the sinful act. . . . This may happen on the part of the ignorance itself, because, to wit, this ignorance is voluntary. . . . For such like negligence renders the ignorance itself voluntary and sinful, provided it be about matters one is bound and able to know.[2]

Thomas cites St. Augustine, upon whose work Aquinas's thinking drew, with the statement about willful ignorance: "*Hoc est peccatum quo tenentur cuncta peccata*" (This is the sin which comprehends all other sins).

Liberty University is not a thirteenth century Catholic university. It's Protestant and fundamentalist. It prides itself on its knowledge of the Bible.

But don't we have to suppose that somewhere in that auditorium in Lynchburg, there was a professor who cringed? Someone there who resonated with the old student at the University of Paris? Someone who thought that telling young professing Christians to arm themselves was a deliberate act of willful ignorance, a sin against faith, the sin that comprehends all others? Someone who knew Matthew 26:52 by heart—Jesus's words to Peter when Peter cut off the high priest's servant's ear at his arrest: "Put away your sword. Those who live by the sword will perish by the sword"—and wanted to scream out loud about willful ignorance?

2. Aquinas, *Summa Theologica I–II*, 145–46.

Willful Ignorance

> Nothing in all the world is
> more dangerous than
> sincere ignorance and
> conscientious stupidity.
>
> —Martin Luther King Jr.[1]

Ours is increasingly a time that wallows in the mire of purposeful ignorance.

Ignorance is one thing. *Willful* ignorance is another. Willful ignorance knows but chooses not to know, or it knows it does not know but acts as though it does. Willful ignorance proffers claims that it either knows are untrue or that it cannot make because it really does not know. Its claims, in either case, are bogus and its speech eats away the common fabric of respectful discourse and action.

Thomas Aquinas wrote about this in his *Summa Theologica* (1274 CE), the masterpiece and fountainhead of scholastic theology continuing into our own time. St. Thomas Aquinas asked whether ignorance can be the cause of sin.

1. King, "Letter from Birmingham Jail," April 16, 1963. https://www.africa.upenn.edu/Articles_Gen/Letter_Birmingham.html.

> It is clear that not every kind of ignorance is the cause of a sin, but that alone which removes the knowledge which would prevent the sinful act. . . . This may happen on the part of the ignorance itself, because, to wit, this ignorance is voluntary, either *directly*, as when a man wishes of set purpose to be ignorant of certain things that he may sin the more freely; or indirectly, as when a man, through stress of work or other occupations, neglects to acquire the knowledge which would restrain him from sin. For such like negligence renders the ignorance itself voluntary and sinful, provided it be about matters one is bound and able to know.[2]

In our time, the word "freedom" has become the chief weapon of those who wish to sin more freely, ignoring what they know. Presidential candidates declare boldly and angrily that "we're going to take our freedom back from government!" by defeating a sitting black president they regard as a closet socialist. Those who speak such sentences are ignorant, misinformed, and woefully mistaken about the nature of freedom, or else *willfully* ignorant, preying upon the equally ignorant or willfully ignorant electorate they seek to rally to their cause.

In America today willful ignorance is on parade in state and national capitols. But it didn't arrive in these capitols by itself. We elected partisan screamers who willfully ignore and, worse, directly attack, the portions of knowledge that do not suit their voluntary purpose—the will to power.

This is a dangerous time. We are easy prey to simple answers. One would hope that those who pray would not fall prey to the claims of willful ignorance, the use of such words as freedom in ways that turn one of our many values into the only value—turn it into a god before which we genuflect.

The shrill voice of the religious and political right in America sounds eerily familiar to those who remember the rise of the German Third Reich. The rise of the Nazi Party happened because the German people chose to disbelieve what they knew to be true and blamed the nation's anxious condition and terrible economic woes

2. Aquinas, *Summa Theologica I-II*, 145–46.

on government itself. Arguably the most sophisticated, highly educated culture of its time, its people inexplicably followed a mad man. They consented to the idea of a Germany purified of the non-Aryan Jews, gays, gypsies, leftists, and leftist sympathizers, though few of them, including Hitler himself, met the qualifications of the Reich's imagined Aryan super race. A people who were antigovernment blamed the Weimar Republic and minority scapegoats for the nation's ills, resulting in totalitarian government.

I hear again the angry voice of fascism and pray that in these hard times the American public and those who lead or who aspire to lead us will leave the history of willful ignorance in the Holocaust Museum and in the silent chambers of Auschwitz.

When a candidate talks about taking back our freedom, ask what freedom s/he is advocating—freedom *from* what and freedom *for* what? Freedom from government? Freedom from socialist programs like Social Security, Medicare, and Medicaid? Freedom for each of us to fend for our own health? Freedom to go it alone without a safety net? Freedom from taxes? Freedom from government that would return clean soil, water, and air to the unregulated industries whose pollution created the need for government regulation? Freedom for big oil, big gas, and big coal to profit while oil, mud, and poison spew from *Deepwater Horizon* in the Gulf of Mexico and the earth's crust is fracked by private coal and gas companies free from the environmental safeguards of the Environmental Protection Agency?

Placed under the scrutiny of a public that refuses to be willfully ignorant, the loud shouts of demagoguery will be swept up by the vacuum of a citizenry schooled in due diligence. And the United States of America, refusing to wallow in the mire of purposeful ignorance, will be a nation of which Thomas Aquinas, and we ourselves, can be proud.

The Anguished Heart of God

One Hebrew word for "god" was "jah."
(It was a time of many words
for god–and many gods.) To say
"hallel" was for all to sing praise,
so HALLELUJAH meant "Praise God!"
(or "Thanks to you, oh God!"—for some
words could be truly translated
more than one way.)
And so, a Psalm, or Song, that offered thanks or praise
might well be paired with a lament:
a cry of pain from one who prays
for help, relief, from gods who sent
disaster. (But, of course, some Psalms
wisely acknowledged that some wrongs
were caused by those who sang the songs!)
There is a Psalm for each one of our days.

—Steve Shoemaker[1]

1. Shoemaker, "A Song for Each Kind of Day."

The Anguished Heart of God

"Now the earth was corrupt in God's sight. It was full of violence," wrote the Genesis writer, introducing the story of Noah and the flood. "The LORD was grieved that he had made man and His heart was full of pain" (Gen 6).

Elie Wiesel, the great novelist and survivor of the Holocaust, was familiar with God's anguish. In his book *Four Hasidic Masters*, he wrote a tribute to a famous Hassidic Jewish rabbi known affectionately as "Rebbe" Barukh:

> The beauty of Rebbe Barukh is that he could speak of faith not as opposed to anguish but as part of it. "Faith and the abyss are next to one another," he told his disciple. "I would even say: one within the other. True faith lies beyond questions; true faith comes after it has been challenged."[2]

There is more than enough anguish across the world to challenge faith. But only faith that has faced the questions—only a faith that understands it is not apart from anguish—is faith as "the courage to be."

Preparing for a trip to Paris in June 2016, we rented an apartment through Airbnb. Opening the apartment, we were struck immediately by the bookcases lining the walls of the long entrance hallway, the living room, dining room, and bedrooms. Some of the books stood out as particularly beautiful—sections of beautiful red leather-bound volumes with gold Arabic calligraphy on their bindings.

Tucked away among the books was an award recognition from the University of the Philippines thanking Abdelwahab Meddeb, professor of comparative literature at the University of Paris, for his wise counsel and assistance in creating an atmosphere of mutual respect and peaceful discourse among the different religions and diverse cultures of the people of the Philippines.

We were staying in the home of Tunisian-born professor, Sufi poet, and novelist who has published twenty books in French.

2. Wiesel, *Four Hasidic Masters*, 59.

Three of them have been translated into English: *The Malady of Islam*, *Talismano*, and *Islam and the Challenge of Civilization*.

We learned from his daughter that Professor Meddeb had died in March 2014, two months after being diagnosed with stage four cancer. After 9/11 he had devoted his writing and lecturing to a Koranic critique of Islamist extremism and the violence rooted in a fatally flawed reading of the holy book he loved.

An open carton of books lay in a corner of the bedroom floor, filled with copies of *Abdelwahab Meddeb: le proche et le lointain* ("the near and the far"), published in Meddeb's honor two months before our arrival. Among the many tributes in French was an English entry from Pierre Joris at the University of Albany. Meddeb's "moral stance," he wrote, "was best expressed by the words of Ibn Arabi":

> I believe in the religion of love; whatever direction its caravan may take—for love is my religion and faith.[3]

Back in the States, when Steve Shoemaker learned we were staying in Meddeb's apartment, he made the connection with the professor's English translator, whom he had interviewed on *Keepin' the Faith*.[4] Within hours an email appeared from the translator at the University of Illinois:

> His writings can be very esoteric, since his interest in Islam spanned so many continents and cultures (hence the title of his radio program, "cultures" with an "s." . . . I almost think it was a good thing he didn't live to see the terrible violence that struck his beloved Paris these recent years. It would have broken his heart to see the evil done in the name of Islam in the city he so loved. He also believed strongly in the secular values of France—he was of that generation—and in the possibility of an Islamic reform coming out of the communities of European Muslims. How sad that exactly the opposite is

3. Manar, "Abdelwahab Meddeb," in *Abdelwahab Meddeb*, 53–56.

4. A weekly Sunday evening radio interview program on WILL.AM, hosted by Steve Shoemaker.

> happening, French Muslims are being radicalized and are filling mosques and prisons.[5]

Saturday morning, two French soldiers stand guard twenty feet to the left of the Meddebs' apartment building. With automatic weapons held tight against their chests, they are guarding the synagogue next door on Shabbat.

> Now the earth was corrupt in God's sight. It was full of violence. The LORD was grieved that he had made man and His heart was full of pain.[6]

We cannot hear the singing from inside the guarded synagogue, but we hear the distant echoes of Rebbe Barukh, "faith lives next to the abyss," and of Ibn Arabi, "I believe in the religion of love; whatever direction its caravan may take—for love is my religion and faith." Standing on holy ground on a Paris street where faith lived and lives next to the abyss, we take off our shoes, knowing that, though the bush is burning, it will never be consumed.

5. Used by permission of the translator.

6. Ge 6:5.

Only One Sin
Exceptionalism

The human race thinks it can go on
with all its Narcissistic human
normalities, of war, of politics,
of religion, and that somehow
the vast other side of the picture
will look after itself. So, in
opting for "himself as conscious,"
man is opting for an ultimate
solitude. And ultimate solitude
is death. It is to be cut off from
the tree of life, and to wither.

—Sebastian Moore, OSB[1]

Kosuke Koyama moved to Minneapolis following retirement from his teaching position at Union Theological Seminary in the city of New York. His friends called him Ko.

I had known Dr. Koyama only by reputation: John D. Rockefeller Jr. professor emeritus of world Christianity; cutting-edge Asian liberation theologian and theological educational leader in

1. Moore, *The Crucified Jesus Is No Stranger*, 69–70.

Thailand, Singapore, New Zealand, and the United States; author of *Water Buffalo Theology, No Handle on the Cross, Three Mile an Hour God, Mt. Fuji and Mt. Sinai,* among others. He was a pioneer in Buddhist-Christian dialogue and interreligious action, a spellbinding keynote speaker at the Fifth Assembly of the World Council of Churches in Nairobi, Kenya.

The friendship that developed between us—it includes mentors and those they mentor, great minds and ordinary ones, people of stature and those who look up to them, the wise and the less wise—was uniquely impactful because my father had been an Army Air Force chaplain on Saipan and Guam in World War II. During the March 1945, Allied firebombing of Tokyo, the bombs came from my father's B-29 air base.

My father rarely spoke about the war. When we asked him for stories about the war, a deep sullenness would sweep over him. Now, after my father's passing, I was learning from Koyama what the war had meant to him, a fifteen-year-old Japanese boy being baptized in Tokyo while the bombs dropped all around his church.

The pastor who baptized him took his face in his hands and charged him: "Kosuke, you are a disciple of Jesus Christ. You must love your neighbors . . . even the Americans."

For the rest of his life Koyama pursued the daunting question of what neighbor-love means. Who is the enemy? Who is the neighbor? Are they one and the same?

Late in his life, he shared over lunch in a sushi restaurant that he had come to the conclusion there is only one sin: exceptionalism. It struck me as strange, but right at the time. Can one really reduce the meaning and scope of sin to exceptionalism? What is exceptionalism? Why is it sinful?

At the time of our discussion, the phrase "American exceptionalism"—the claim that the United States is exceptional among nations—was making its way into the news. It was this view that led to the invasions and wars in Afghanistan and Iraq under the illusion that the Afghanis and the Iraqis would welcome the Americans with open arms as liberators.

In the language and actions of this American belligerence Koyama heard the latest form of an old claim that had brought such devastation on the Japanese people as well as the people of the world. The voices from the White House, the State Department, and the Department of Defense, though they spoke English instead of Japanese, sounded familiar, impervious to criticism and calls for restraint on the nation's military and economic adventures.

On Hiroshima Day, August 6, 2006, Koyama addressed a small crowd at the Peace Garden in Minneapolis at the exact hour Little Boy incinerated Hiroshima. His voice rang with a quiet authority that comes from the depths of experience. Here's an excerpt from that speech:

> During the war (1941–45), the Japanese people were bombarded by the official propaganda that Japan is the divine nation, for the emperor is divine. The word "divine" was profusely used. This was Japanese wartime "dishonest religion," or shall we call it "mendacious theology"? This "god-talk" presented an immature god who spoke only Japanese and was undereducated about other cultures and international relations. Trusting in this parochial god, Japan destroyed itself.
>
> Dear friends, do not trust a god who speaks only English, and has no understanding of Arabic or Islamic culture and history. If you follow such a small-town god you may be infected with the poison of exceptionalism: "I am okay. You are not okay." For the last 5,000 years the self-righteous passion of "I am okay. You are not okay" has perpetuated war and destruction. War "has never been and it will never be able to solve international conflicts," says Pope John Paul II.

Two paragraphs later, Koyama spoke in terms that refer to the policy of drones and other advanced military technology:

> In spite of the remarkable advances humanity has made in science/technological [*sic*], our moral and spiritual

> growth has been stunted. Humankind seems addicted to destruction even with nuclear weapons and biological weapons. Today there are 639 million small arms actively present in the world (*National Catholic Reporter*, June 30, 2006). Fear propaganda always kills hope. Violence is called sacrifice. Children killed in war are cruelly called a part of the "collateral damage."[2]

Years later on Hiroshima Day, I wish I could break bread with Ko and my father, to discuss the meaning of it all and share with my father the haiku poems published in the *New York Times* following Ko's death, written in his honor by his colleague at Union Theological Seminary, Peggy Shriver—testaments to hope in belligerent times:

Smiling East-West spirit,
You move with sun and Son,
Shining Peace on us.

Like a child piling blocks
Your words construct new dreams,
Towering poet.

Gentle and strong, as trees
Bend gracefully in wind,
You stand—and I bow.[3]

2. Kosuke Koyama, unpublished speech, August 6, 2006, Minneapolis, Minnesota.

3. Shriver, *The Dancers of Riverside Park*, 99.

The Economy

Only *One* House

In the long term,
the economy and the environment
are the same thing.
If it's unenvironmental
it is uneconomical.
That is a rule of nature.

—Mollie H. Beattie[1]

Economics is about a household and how to manage it. The household is a family, a state, a nation, a planet.

The English word "economy" comes from the Greek word *οἶκος* [oikos]—the word for house. The word "economics" derives from the Greek word *οἰκονομία* [oikonomia]—the management of a household. Before anything else, economics is a perspective, a frame of reference. Before it decides anything about household management, it knows that there is only one house. Good

1. Quoted in Ted Gup, "Woman of the Woods." Mollie Beattie (1947–1996) was the first woman appointed as director of the United States Fish and Wildlife Service. With degrees in forestry and public administration, she was a beekeeper whose view of the planet seemed to echo Marcus Aurelius' (121–180 CE) aphorism: "That which is not good for the beehive cannot be good for the bees" (Marcus Aurelius, *Meditations*). The planet is our beehive.

household management—*good economics*—pays attention to the well-being of the entire house and all its residents.

In America and elsewhere across the world, we are coming to realize that the planet itself is one house. What happens in one room of the house—one family, one city, one nation—affects what happens everywhere in the house. Philosopher and theologian Paul Tillich (1886–1965) caught a clear sense of it when he wrote that "[humankind] and nature belong together in their created glory—in their tragedy and in their salvation."[2]

The essential question of economics is not about systems: capitalism, communism, socialism, or anything else. The question is spiritual, philosophical, and ethical: whether we believe there is only one *οἶκος*. The secondary consideration is how best to manage the house in ways that respect the dignity of all its residents and the fragile web of nature without which the house of the living would not exist.

Very often what we call "economics" is not economics. It's something else. It assumes something else. When we forget what an economy and economics really are, we enshrine greed as the essential virtue, ignoring and imperiling everyone else and everything in the one house in which we all live.

If it's unenvironmental, it is uneconomical. The planet is our beehive. There is only one house.

2. Quote engraved on Tillich's headstone in Tillich Park, New Harmony, Indiana.

Climate Change and the Nations

I came to see myself as growing
out of the earth like the other native
animals and plants. I saw my body
and my daily motions as brief
coherences and articulations of
the energy of the place, which would
fall back into it like the leaves of autumn.
In this awakening there has been a
good deal of pain.

—Wendell Berry[1]

"The Philippines envoy to the UN climate change conference has issued an emotional announcement that he will go on hunger strike unless talks lead to a 'meaningful outcome.'"[2]

Naderev "Yeb" Saño[3] was not the only one fasting. So was a lifelong friend in Pennsylvania. Carolyn and I were in kindergar-

1. Berry, "A Native Hill," in *The Art of the Commonplace*, 7–8.

2. Withnall, "Typhoon Haiyan."

3. Saño later resigned from the Philippines Climate Change Commission, preferring to work outside the system with interfaith advocacy groups. In November 2015, he led the People's Pilgrimage of Our Voices, a sixty-day walk

ten together. Our families were best friends. We grew up in each other's living rooms. We went to the same church. Went to Sunday school and Confirmation together. Graduated from high school together. Our parents retired to the same retirement community in Cornwall, Pennsylvania, where one after the other they each came to the end of their lives concerned about the shape of the future. Carolyn and I come by it naturally, I suppose. The Kidder DNA and the Stewart DNA, although infinitesimally different, are like the DNA of the entire human species: essentially the same.

What happens to the human species if the scientists have it right? How do we care for each other across the planet—one species in the Philippines, Poland, the Netherlands, Argentina, and the United States—while facing the daunting changes that are coming? If we believe that we are our brothers' and sisters' keepers, what changes will we make individually and together to exercise that responsibility?

Carolyn and Yeb have decided to fast until the meeting in Warsaw leads to a meaningful outcome. Fasting is not for everyone, although I can't help wonder what impact it would have if there was a fast across the world that spoke louder than words to the national representatives gathered this week by the United Nations in Warsaw, Poland.

In place of fasting this morning I looked again at the strange little book of Haggai in Hebrew Scripture, and what did I see? A civil leader named Zerubbabel and a religious leader named Joshua trying to lead their people during a time of colonial occupation. We, too, live under colonial occupation—the occupation of international greed and neglect of the planet, its people, and the environment. Perhaps Carolyn and Yeb are like the prophet Haggai, whose term of ministry was less than four months.

> The word of the LORD[4] came a second time to Haggai on the twenty-fourth day of the month: Speak to Zerub-

from Rome to Paris in time for the UN Climate Change Summit.

4. When the word "Lord" appears in small caps, it translates the name that is beyond speaking aloud—YHWH—the *mysterium tremendum et fascinans* beyond human controlling. Because the name is only consonants, it permits

> babel, governor of Judah, saying, I am about to shake the heavens and the earth, and to overthrow the throne of kingdoms; I am about to destroy the strength of the kingdoms of the nations. . . . On that day, says the Lord of hosts, I will take you, O Zerubbabel, my servant, . . . and make you like a signet ring; for I have chosen you, says the Lord of hosts. (Hag 2:20–23)

The climate shaking that has driven Yeb and Carolyn to fasting is no respecter of nations. It knows no national boundaries. Nationalist thinking has outlived its time. There is only one people. Only one human species in a wonderful diversity of geography, culture, color, religion, and language. The kingdoms of the nations are gathered today in Warsaw, and one of their representatives from the Philippines is shaking the presumption of all of the thrones. The national delegates bear the equivalent of the king's signet ring to sign and seal agreements and documents on behalf of the modern equivalent of their kings. Sometimes in life a person is like a signet ring for a new order, a man for our time like Naderev Yeb Saño.

translation as "I am who I am" or "I will be who I will be."

The Wall Street Tattler

> Over the last 12 months I have seen five different managing directors refer to their own clients as "muppets," sometimes in internal e-mails.
>
> —Greg Smith[1]

How could he do this? Is Greg Smith a tattler? Or, perhaps, a Judas?

How could one of Wall Street's own go to the *New York Times*[2] to denounce the company's culture? "'He just took a howitzer and blew the entire firm away,' said Larry Doyle, president of Greenwich Investment Management."[3]

According to the *Los Angeles Times* article, Goldman Sachs CEO Lloyd Blankfein suggests that Mr. Smith is "a disgruntled employee." William Cohan, author of *Money and Power: How Goldman Sachs Came to Rule the World*, says "there are lots of disgruntled people who leave Wall Street, and they don't do this" (i.e., open their mouths). "What I'm hearing," said Cohan, "is sour

1. Smith, "Why I am Leaving Goldman Sachs." Greg Smith was Goldman Sachs's executive director and head of its United States equity derivative business in Europe, the Middle East, and Africa.

2. Ibid.

3. Hamilton and Popper, "Goldman Sachs Executive's Parting."

grapes. You just pigged out at the trough for 12 years and you don't have enough sense to keep your mouth shut."[4]

Keeping one's mouth shut is the name of the game on Wall Street.

Conscience may have its place so long as you keep it to yourself. You can have a conscience on Wall Street, just don't exercise it. You are part of an elite gang. Whether on the street corners of impoverished neighborhoods like Watts in Los Angeles and Bedford-Stuyvesant in New York City, or in the center of the crony capitalism that is Wall Street, gang members don't rat on other gang members. If you don't like it, swallow hard and keep your mouth shut.

"It makes me ill how callously people talk about ripping their clients off," said Greg Smith. "Over the 12 months I have seen five different managing directors refer to their own clients as 'muppets,' sometimes in internal emails."

Goldman's rebuttal to Mr. Smith's statement—"We disagree with the views expressed, which we don't think reflect the way we run our business"—hardly rings of a strong denial.

It's a rare thing for a spokesperson at a corporation with the best legal counsel in the world to say anything other than a flat-out denial. "We don't think" sets up the issue as a matter of perception, not fact. It's Goldman's perceptions of itself versus Mr. Smith's disgruntled perception.

Mr. Smith's refusal to live by the Wall Street gang code of conduct will lead to a barrage of attacks on his character calculated to divert the public's attention from an institution that eats people's investments and life savings to the tattler who is without integrity.

Goldman understands that for most of us the world is personal, not institutional. We don't like tattletales and turncoats, disgruntled employees who never learned the lesson of kindergarten that you never tattle on your friends. You don't go running home to tell Momma. Part of the code of the playground is not to tell. It's also the gang code.

4. Ibid.

What's even more unusual in this case is that Greg Smith dealt in derivatives. Derivatives—a complex form of financial market gambling so convoluted that even the people who manage them can't explain how they work—were at the center of the Wall Street meltdown in 2008. They were legal then. They are legal now. Goldman Sachs and the rest of the Wall Street gang of crony capitalists are still calling the shots with the highest paid Washington lobbyists money can buy.

Greg Smith is a Wall Street Judas, but he didn't betray his gang with a kiss. He blew them away with a howitzer.

How could he do this? Why didn't the executive who ate at the pig trough for twelve years just quietly kiss and say good-bye? Why did he make his money and then break the code? Unless, unlike so many of those who were taught not to tattle, Greg Smith couldn't live with himself and finally decided not to run home to tell Momma but to instead run to the *New York Times*. He'll never again be allowed on the playground.

Sorrow Floats

Concepts, like individuals, have their histories
and are just as incapable of withstanding
the ravages of time as individuals. But in and
through all this they retain a kind of homesickness
for the scenes of their childhood.

—Soren Kierkegaard[1]

"Sorrow floats."

Perhaps the line from John Irving's *The Hotel New Hampshire* in which Sorrow, the stuffed family dog preserved by a taxidermist, floats to the surface of the lake after a plane crash, helps explain what is happening in America.

Something dear to the American family died in September and October 2008. Prior to the series of chilling events of that period, most of us had lived with the illusion of relative economic and financial health. Then, suddenly, Sorrow was rushed to the emergency room for government resuscitation.

Since then our memories of that pre-October 2008 world have taken a turn that families often take at funerals when the

1. Kierkegaard, *The Concept of Irony*, introduction. Kierkegaard was a Danish philosopher-theologian.

eulogies bear little resemblance to the reality of the deceased. We're quarreling over what was real and what is mythical reconstruction.

Following the plane wreck that takes the lives of the Berry family parents in Irving's *The Hotel New Hampshire*, the stuffed family pet bobs to the surface of the lake, floating among the wreckage. Sorrow floats. So does the thing we lost last fall.

WHAT DIED? A RULING ASSUMPTION

What died last year was the ruling assumption that an unregulated free-market system was the best way to organize an economy and that laissez-faire capitalism is democracy's natural ally. The market almost crashed. It didn't crash only because the federal government intervened to prevent a repeat of the crash of 1929. Sometime between mid-September and October 7, when Congress passed its bill to stabilize the financial markets, the myth of the virtue of deregulated capitalism died. It was stuffed by the taxidermy of government intervention, but it still floats.

When a conviction or a myth dies, it doesn't go away. It continues to bob to the surface. Sometimes, as in the case of the Berry family, the old dog is much easier to love after it is dead. Sorrow—obese, lethargic, and persistently flatulent in its old age—no longer waddles through the dining room to foul the air and ruin everyone's dinner. In the public psyche, the unpleasant memories of the real life Sorrow give way to the stuffed Sorrow, a thing of nostalgia that lives on . . . even after it's dead, and long after the plane has crashed.

OVER AND OVER, WE FORGET

Sorrow and its old illusions float every time the reconstructed memory, forgetting the real Sorrow, barks about "socialism." Sorrow floats every time we shout each other down in town-hall meetings. Sorrow floats every time nostalgia forgets that it was only by government intervention with our tax dollars that Sorrow is still around. Sorrow floats every time we forget the voracious appetite, unscrupulous predatory practices, insatiable greed, and obesity that led to the deaths of the Lehmann Brothers, Merrill Lynch, and Bear Stearns, not to mention insurance giant AIG and all the banks that had taken the plunge into a market of deregulated derivatives and mortgages that led to the epidemic of home foreclosures, bankruptcies, pension-fund collapses, and job losses. Sorrow, the old dog that failed us, still floats and still barks a year after the crash when the mind forgets and nostalgia remembers a system we thought was working in our interest.

Old ideas and convictions die hard. The powerful economic forces that grew fat during the years when government was viewed as the people's enemy will stoke the fires of public anxiety and anger, taking advantage of the floating Sorrow that reminds us of something we love more in retrospect than the day it died of its own obesity.

The American Oligarchy—4/29/10

Experience demands that man is the only
animal which devours his own kind, for I can apply
no milder term to the general prey of the rich on the poor.

—Thomas Jefferson[1]

America is living stormy Monday, but the pulpit
is preaching happy Sunday.
The world is experiencing the Blues, and
pulpiteers are dispensing excessive doses
of non-prescription prosaic sermons with
several ecclesiastical and theological side effects.
The church is becoming a place where
Christianity is nothing more than
capitalism in drag.

—Otis Moss III[2]

1. Thomas Jefferson to Edward Carrington, January 16, 1787, in Jefferson, *Papers*, 11:48–49.

2. Moss, *Blue Note Preaching*, 4.

We do not live in a democracy; we live in an oligarchy—"government by the few, especially despotic power exercised by a small and privileged group for corrupt or selfish purposes."[3] I've been waiting for people in high places to say it.

Goldman Sachs executives' testimony Tuesday before the Senate Permanent Subcommittee on Investigations[4] brought the elephant into the living room, but the name of this species of government remains unspoken for understandable reasons.

A democratic republic is a constitutional form of government where the people rule through their elected representatives gathered in deliberative bodies. The faces and voices of Goldman Sachs's executives demonstrated the intransigent arrogance of the private institutional concentration of the wealth and power of deregulated capitalism.

The matter is growing more serious.

The "small and privileged group" that operates corruptly and selfishly knows that elections are bought and sold in America. No one gets elected without big money.

A CIRCUS FOR THE MASSES

Those who derive such economic advantage from Wall Street know that much of what's happening in these hearings is a circus—a public show for the masses. They knew going in that the senators would take turns shouting at them about greed and unregulated derivatives and the fraud that led to the home-mortgage crisis and the near meltdown of the economy. They knew that for a day or two the senators would look and act like the public servants we elected them to be, but more important, they knew that two or three days later that they'd still be in charge of the country because they own the electoral system and those we elect.

3. *Encyclopedia Britannica*, s.v. "oligarchy," https://www.britannica.com/topic/oligarchy.

4. See Senate Permanent Subcommittee on Investigations, "Wall Street and the Financial Crisis."

This small and privileged group owns both political parties. While Republicans scream about socialism and Democrats talk more like regulators, but neither party dares take a swipe at the trunk that feeds them.

The later Roman emperors knew that political power is a game of economic security and diversionary entertainment. "Bread and circuses"—a phrase coined by the Roman poet Juvenal around 100 CE—lamented that a once vigorous republic anchored in thoughtful public debate about national life had gone off to the circuses, leaving public policy to the few. Throw the people some bread and give them entertainment and they'll be happy—because they're stupid.

LOOK CLOSER—AT THE SNEER

Today we watched Senate investigative hearings at which we saw the senators mad as hell and Goldman Sachs's Lloyd Blankfein and Fabrice Tourre frying on the hot seat. But look closer at the sneer on their faces and listen to the bark in their voices that seem to say to the senators and everyone who's watching, "You can put us on public trial to cleanse your own conscience for a moment or to convince an angry public that you're doing something, but you and we both know that tomorrow you're going to need our campaign contributions to get reelected. The hearing makes good public theater, but tomorrow and the day after, we'll still be running the show. This is an oligarchy!"

If the electorate of a constitutional democratic republic substitutes short-term security (bread) and the diversions of entertainment (circuses) for the hard work of vigorous public debate and the search for reality and truth, the elephant in our living room will continue to grow without ever being named or discussed.

Truth alone has the power to set us free. Until the truth is told, heard, and hammered home, increasing numbers of us will find ourselves on the street because there was no longer any room left for us in the house we thought we owned.

Mary of Occupy

He has shown strength with his arm;
he has scattered the proud
in the thoughts of their hearts.
He has brought down the powerful
from their thrones, and lifted up the lowly;
he has filled the hungry with good things,
and sent the rich away empty.

—LUKE 1:53–55

In other cultures, and other times, the young woman would be called a peasant. But here and now, she is a protester, one of a dwindling number of ragged young people on the government plaza. She moves among the occupier sleeping bags and protest signs in the cold of winter, singing her song of hope and joy.

She makes no demands, which is confusing to some. Hers is a different way: a bold announcement that the old order, symbolized by Wall Street, is already finished. Her purity and her message are impervious to the game of demand-and-response that serves only to tweak and tinker with the old system of greed and financial violence.

She simply affirms the great new thing that will come to pass. To her it is more real than much of what she sees.

A song like hers is being sung this season in churches throughout the world. The song rejoices in a new world order about to be born. The "same old, same old" world, the one defined by who's up and who's down, by social pride and social humiliation, by the overfed and underfed, by extremes of extravagant wealth and poverty—that world is over. The mountains of greed are brought down and the pits of desperation are raised up to the plain.

The song celebrated in churches is the *Magnificat*, the Song of Mary, a composition of the Gospel of Luke. It has special meaning to Christians who believe that Mary bore in her womb the savior of us all. But the Luke story also serves as a metaphor for the compassionate character of a new society about to be born.

"My spirit rejoices in God my Savior," sings this peasant girl living in the time of the Roman Empire's foreign occupation. She is full of the one who "has scattered the proud in the imaginations of their hearts," who "has brought down the mighty from their thrones, and has lifted up those of low degree," the leveling God of mercy and justice.

Imagine for a moment an opera house. At one end of the stage stands Mary, the voice of prophetic madness, her tender voice softly rejoicing in the hope growing inside her. At the other end stands a massive chorus, in tuxedos and gowns, thundering its hymn of praise for the market, for its grandeur, for the preservation of the status quo.

"He has filled the hungry with good things," the girl sings, "and the rich he has sent empty away." Her voice cannot compete in volume. But in its clarity, it drowns out the mighty chorus.

As Mary's song is read in churches this Sunday, some anonymous girl will slip unnoticed into the back pew. She will listen to the reading of Luke's *Magnificat*, and she will hope, like Mary, that the world will hear the message.

A Visit with the Deeper Memory

But often, in the world's most crowded streets,
But often, in the din of strife,
There rises an unspeakable desire
After the knowledge of our buried life;
A thirst to spend our fire and restless force
In tracking out our true, original course;
A longing to inquire
Into the mystery of this heart which beats
So wild, so deep in us—to know
Whence our lives come and where they go.

—MATTHEW ARNOLD[1]

Visiting with a ninety-one-year-old friend with terminal cancer, the discussion turns to her final wishes. Mary is a child psychologist by profession, a retired professor whose pioneering work with children at the University of Minnesota and Minneapolis's Children's Hospital is a legacy that will remain long after she is gone.

1. Arnold, "The Buried Life," in *Empedocles on Etna*, 45–54.

Raised in a strict Calvinist Christian tradition in Grand Rapids, Michigan, the faith she inherited from her home had been shipwrecked many decades ago. But she had found herself in the quiet gatherings of the Quaker meetings, the respectful naturalist spirituality of St. Francis of Assisi, and indigenous American spiritual traditions that see the sacred in the cirrus clouds, the fluttering of a leaf, the chickadee at the bird feeder on the deck, or the circling of an eagle overhead.

When her husband Doug died three years before, Mary and their five adult children gathered privately to inter Doug's ashes in a small opening in the woods on their farm near Wabasha. Doug, like Mary, is legendary in Minnesota, in a different sort of way, as the street lawyer with the ponytail, the cofounder and director of the Legal Rights Center, Inc. at the urging of the American Indian Movement (AIM) and African-American civil rights leaders in Minneapolis, the trusted intermediary between the federal troops and the AIM members at the Wounded Knee occupation in 1973—Dennis and Russell Means, Clyde Bellecourt Jr., Leonard Peltier, Dennis Banks, et al.

The day the family buried Doug's ashes in that small opening in the woods, they marked the spot with stones pointing north, east, south, and west—the four directions pointing to the four corners of the earth. Early the following morning—the day we would publicly celebrate Doug's life—one of Doug and Mary's grieving daughters walked into the woods for some quiet time in the wooded glen. To her great surprise, a bald eagle was sitting very still in the center of the four stones above her father's ashes.

I asked Mary at the time what she made of that. With great respect, she paused, said she didn't know and something to the effect that native peoples seem to be in touch with mysteries that elude the rest of us. Her statement struck me at the time because in our talks about death and dying, she had always indicated that she believed that life is lived between the boundary limits of birth and death. The eagle sitting on Doug's ashes in that tiny circle in the woods didn't seem to convince her of something beyond the grave, but she held a kind of sacred openness to the possibility, a respectful not-knowing about human destiny, the universe, and our place in it.

Now, three years after Doug's death, we sit together as we often have over a lunch of shrimp, salad, and fresh bread at the table that looks out at the bird feeders on the deck of the old converted mill on the farm up the hill from Wabasha. Three of her five children are here.

Missy asks Mary whether she has told me her plans for her service when the end comes. There is a long silence as Mary goes away to some private inner place—some wooded glen where no one else can go. Her eyes are distant, dreamlike, looking off to some far off place, sorting through her long spiritual journey to fetch the right words out of the forest of ninety-one years of experience and memory.

Finally, she speaks—softly. Quietly. Deliberately. "I want you to do the prayer, and I want the benediction."

"What kind of prayer?" I ask.

She gives me a quizzical look, as if I should know.

"Something classical with the gravitas of tradition?"

"Yes," she says.

"And what kind of benediction?" I ask.

"Blessed are the peacemakers," she says.

"And music. What about music?"

"Oh, yes" she says. "Bach, Mozart, Beethoven . . . and 'Let there be peace on Earth,'" and she wanders off again into that most personal space of the deeper memory where no one else can go. Ninety-one years summed up in four words: "Blessed are the peacemakers" from Jesus's Sermon on the Mount in the Gospel according to Matthew.

She is growing weary now. It's time for her afternoon nap. We say good-bye. I leave this sacred place of Mary's world, get behind the wheel to drive home, turn on the radio, and hear news, so far removed from Mary's world and Jesus's, with all the saber-rattling and the name-calling, and I wish we all could have lunch with Mary or take a walk to the wooded glen where the eagle sat still above Doug's grave at the center of the four corners of the earth.

"Blessed are the meek, for they shall inherit the earth."

Get Off My Corner!

Let us hope and pray that the vast intelligence, imagination, humor, and courage will not fail us. Either we learn a new language of empathy and compassion, or the fire this time will consume us.

—Cornel West[1]

I'm sitting calmly in my office when the phone rings. It's a parishioner who lives near the downtown post office. "I don't know what's happening," she says, "but there's some kind of ruckus on the corner. There's some kind of booth on the corner."

I drive to the post office. I park the car half a block away and see a large booth on the street corner. The woman handing out literature is yelling at a man who's crossing the street, and he's yelling back. I can't hear what they're saying until I draw closer. A man crossing the street to get away from the booth is shouting over his shoulder: "You're not only anti-Semitic! You're anti-American!"

The booth features an eight-foot-tall photograph of the president of the United States. But this is no ordinary photograph. There's a mustache imposed on President Obama's picture, the mustache of Adolf Hitler and a call for his impeachment, "Dump Obama!"

1. West, *Race Matters*, 13.

I approach the booth. "Just another Jew," says the woman.

"What's happening?" I ask.

She slides a flyer across the counter.

"Read it!" she says.

The flyer has the same picture of the president. I put my finger on the mustache.

"You don't want to hear what we have to say. You're a spy!" she says as she steps backward, tilts her head in the air, and bellows out the tune: "O beautiful for spacious skies, For amber waves of grain, For purple mountain majesty, Above the fruited plain. America! America! God shed His grace on thee." But before she sings the last line of the stanza—"and crown thy good with brotherhood"—she stops and orders me away. "Get off my corner!"

She is carrying the message of Lyndon LaRouche, a perpetual candidate for president whose only consistency over a long checkered history of ideological swings on the political spectrum is the lava of righteous rage.

The behavior of the woman at the post office, like that of the Florida pastor whose threat to burn Korans nearly set the world on fire several years ago, is bizarre. But the rage she expresses is not unique to her. Because it is so outrageous, it shines a light into the darkness of the widespread incivility of our time, an incivility that erupts from a core conviction hidden below the surface of our consciousness—American exceptionalism.

We're street brawling over what kind of America we will be, and "can't we all just get along"—the plea of Rodney King as he witnessed the Los Angeles riots following the "innocent" verdict exonerating the police officers whose beatings of him had been aired repeatedly on national television—is long forgotten. We're dividing ourselves into true believers and heretics, patriots and traitors, suspicious of each other all the way to the White House.

The horrors of powerful religious dogmatism led the founders of the new American republic to write into the US Constitution that there would be no established religion. The American republic would be a secular republic with freedom of religious expression. It would not be a theocracy.

As the new nation was being conceived, demagoguery often replaced politics (i.e., the art of compromise), as it often does now. One does not compromise with the enemy. One eliminates him. Rodney King's plea is regarded as the way of the ill-informed or of cowards, heretics, and anti-Americans.

The volcanic eruptions originate in the collective conviction that the United States is for the chosen people, the messianic people whose job is to eliminate evil within and without in the war of good against evil. It is an idea born of the rape of the Judeo-Christian tradition by nationalism, which installs America as the exception to history, the nation divinely ordained to banish Anne Hutchinson, hang Mary Dyer, and destroy the reputations of thoughtful critics like Pete Seeger in Senator Joseph McCarthy's purge in the 1950s. It's the conviction that America is the exception and that the real America consists of only some of us.

In the unspoken consciousness of our collective memory, "you are the light of the world" becomes the declaration of fact spoken about America, not an itinerant preacher's call to a small band of first-century disciples to persist in the hard politics of love and peace in a time of hate and violence. The ensuing lines from the Sermon on the Mount—"You have heard that it was said, 'You must love your neighbor as yourself,' but I say to you, love your enemy and do good to those who persecute you"—get forgotten, ignored, torn out, blacked out, or sacrificed on the altar of messianic nationalism.

It is even more ironic that those who attack others, including a sitting president, as un-American—i.e., "heretics" who do not bow to the idea of America as the collective messiah of history—scream against government and taxes as enemies, socialist intrusions on their individual freedom to hoard what is theirs. The biblical city is no longer a community of sharing of the wealth and care for the least; it is reshaped as a sandbox of greed and competition where the highest value is my freedom to get and keep what is mine.

The irony is that in the minds and hearts of those who have been raped, "America the beautiful . . . God shed his grace on thee" is no longer a statement of aspiration but of fact. And the prayer "God mend thine every flaw"—the flaws of selfishness and greed, our meanness to each other, our name-calling and stereotyping, our entrenched partisanship, our collective nationalist arrogance—become a distant memory of a censored sentiment. In times like these when ugliness replaces beauty, America the beautiful is, as it always has been, a courageous aspiration and prayer for sanity in the midst of collective madness.

The Return to South Paris

> To come into the presence of the place was to know life and death, and to be near in all your thoughts to laughter and to tears. This would come over you and then pass away, as fragile as a moment of light.
>
> —Wendell Berry[1]

Memory contorts reality. It also redeems it. Take the house at 110 Porter Street for instance, the home my aunt Gertrude, my mother's sister, made for the Smith family in South Paris, Maine. It was home for my aunt, my uncle Bob, and my cousins Alan, Dennis, and Gwen. Once a second home to me, it has become a place of memory. Like lots of things in life, we'd been driven apart by the years. I hadn't seen it in thirty-six years.

I drove by the place when I called back to South Paris for Aunt Gertrude's memorial service. My aunt had sold the house long ago. Seeing the place for the first time after all these years, the sense of grief was palpable. Its size and proportions bore little resemblance to my memory of it, though my cousins said it looked about the same. It was bigger in my memory, more prominent, you

1. Berry, *Jayber Crow*, 205–6.

might say, because of who lived there. But the memory as well as the reality of the place was a mixture of love and sadness.

The house on 110 Porter Street was a fishbowl in a small town where everyone knew—or thought they knew, or wanted to know—everyone else's business, especially a prominent person like Uncle Bob, the judge of Oxford County. It took a strong woman to protect the family on Porter Street. My aunt was that woman.

Uncle Bob and Aunt Gertrude met at the Congregational Church when Bob opened a law office in South Paris after graduation from Harvard Law School. Gertrude was a schoolteacher.

Their first child, Alan, was born with cerebral palsy. Alan never spoke a word; he spoke only with his eyes. My memories of Alan include the immutable daily routine of my aunt and uncle carrying his deadweight body down the stairs in the morning to the kitchen table where they would feed him breakfast; then carrying him to the daybed in the parlor where Alan would spend his day; carrying him back and forth for lunch and dinner; and, at the end of every day, carrying him upstairs to prepare him for bed. Every day . . . without end . . . without a break . . . until Alan was fourteen.

Early in his career, my uncle Bob became the judge of Oxford County. Following long periods when he would slip into the inner horrors of deep darkness, he was diagnosed with bipolar disorder. My aunt Gertrude was the rock that kept the family afloat when Bob was hospitalized, leaving Alan, Dennis, and Gwen to her unaided care. She and Uncle Bob continued to live in the modest house on Porter Street after Alan died and after Dennis and Gwen had left the nest. Uncle Bob died of a cerebral hemorrhage while leading an annual meeting of the Congregational Church of South Paris where he served as the church's lay president and organist for forty-three years. After his death, Aunt Gertrude sold the house and moved to a southern climate.

My cousins have asked me to conduct the memorial service. The family is gathering from across the country to pay our respects—to remember and to celebrate her remarkable life of ninety-nine vigorous years.

Arriving at the Congregational Church—"the Congo church," they call it in South Paris—after all these years, a sense of forlornness falls over me. Like the house on Porter Street, the church looks nothing like what I remember. The hallway walls are bare, with one exception: a framed black-and-white photograph of my uncle as a young man at the organ. "Bob Smith—Organist and Choirmaster (1938–1981)."

An older man I don't recognize approaches me. He looks me in the eye and extends his hand. "Warren," he says. It doesn't ring a bell. "Your cousin . . . Warren," he says. "I guess we've both changed a bit!" Warren is a man of few words with our grandfather Titus's twinkle in his eyes. Our grandfather wasn't much of a talker; he was a doer. So is Warren.

Looking out from behind the pulpit at the gathered community of cousins, relatives, and friends while listening to the organ prelude, my memory drifts back to my uncle Bob. The childhood memories come flooding back. I see the faces that are there and the ones that are there only in memory.

I'm a boy sitting next to Grandpa Titus, his baritone voice bellowing out the hymns as if he and I were the only ones singing. Uncle Bob is at the organ, playing some great classical organ piece by J. S. Bach or Dietrich Buxtehude. Aunt Gertrude and my mother are sitting behind us, trying not to giggle over some irreverent and mischievous behavior from their children—marbles dropped on the floor or a yelp from a poke in the ribs. Or maybe they were swallowing the giggles after a whispered comment by Aunt Gertrude's best friend, Esther Morton, when Ken Gray, the scholarly preacher who looked like Washington Irving's Ichabod Crane from *The Legend of Sleepy Hollow*, straightened his tall body and stretched his long neck sanctimoniously forward or spoke a word that no one but Uncle Bob would know without the help of a dictionary.

I now look out from Ken Gray's pulpit at my cousins Dennis and Gwen, the bald Warren and an astonishingly large number of people who have come to honor the ninety-nine-year-old Gertrude, who delivered Meals on Wheels until the year before she died down in North Carolina. We are gathered here as a community of strangers and exiles gathered in from the diaspora, brought together by the streams of family affection and shared memory. The sights, sounds, and smells of childhood again fill the empty spaces of 110 Porter Street and the Congo Church with a love that cannot be broken by time.

It takes a while to know the meaning of time and not to dread it. Like Jayber Crow in Wendell Berry's novel by the same name, I am seeing the place as I have never seen it before. I long ago left South Paris, but like Jayber Crow I realize that

> I could not be extracted from [South Paris] like a pit from a plum, and . . . it could not be extracted from me; death could not set it and me apart. . . . To come into the presence of the place was to know life and death, and to be near in all your thoughts to laughter and to tears. This would come over you and then pass away, as fragile as a moment of light."[2]

Memory not only contorts reality. It also redeems it.

2. Ibid., 206.

God as Policeman or Lover?

The end of the story is that man the lover is
completely vindicated, justified acquitted.
And that's what the love of God is.
This is the Resurrection, the hatching of man
the lover out of the thick millennial cocoon
of man the sinner.

—SEBASTIAN MOORE[1]

Dom Sebastian Moore (1917–2014), a Benedictine Monk of Downside Abbey, England, is one of our time's more interesting thinkers.

Steeped in the psychology of Carl Jung, the spiritual discipline of the Benedictine Order, the theology of Bernard Lonergan, SJ, and the mimetic theory of Rene Girard, his eyes were penetrating, his vision deep and far-reaching. During a long life of spiritual searching, he wrote in his book *The Inner Loneliness*,

> Once you see the self as naturally self-centered, you deny that the self wants God above all things, and you degrade God from being the fulfiller, the lover, into being the policeman. Paul's conversion, through the stunning vision

1. Moore, *The Inner Loneliness*, 49.

> of Jesus he had on the road to Damascus, was from God the policeman to God the lover."[2]

We met briefly in 1971, at a meeting of area campus ministers in Milwaukee. He was chaplain at Marquette University at the same time I served as campus minister at the University of Wisconsin-Whitewater. Gathered at the Episcopal Campus Ministry Center at the University of Wisconsin-Milwaukee, I wondered who this strange monk was who seemed to observe everyone very closely without saying more than a word or two. I'm not sure I even knew his name. I just knew he was unusual.

Twenty-six years later, during a period of personal and professional turmoil, a therapist mentioned the name Sebastian Moore. I purchased *The Crucified Jesus Is No Stranger* and saw his picture on the jacket. His perspective left me in awe and anchors me still. I've been knocked off my horse on the way to Damascus. Every real conversion is the turning from God the policeman to God the lover.

2. Ibid.

The Bristlecone Pines

> God has cared for these trees,
> saved them from drought, disease,
> and a thousand tempests and floods.
> But he cannot save them from fools.
>
> —John Muir[1]

In *Souls on Fire*, Elie Wiesel tells the story of "*prophetic* madness" challenging the "*collective* madness" that blithely ignores an impending crisis of crop failure. "Good people . . . what is at stake," says the prophetic messenger, "is your life, your survival! The summons falls on deaf ears and the calamity of starvation is not averted." Wiesel concludes, "God loves madmen. They're the only ones he allows near him."[2]

Late in the year of 1964, a young geography student working toward his doctorate came upon a grove of bristlecone pines while doing research on Ice Age glaciers.

Wheeler Peak, on Nevada's eastern border with Utah, reaches an altitude of 13,063 feet with a spectacular glacial cirque on its northeast side. Wheeler Peak cycles through five life zones, from the hot stony desert to alpine tundra, all within a five-mile line.

1. Muir, *Our National Parks*, 365.

2. Wiesel, *Souls on Fire*, 202.

Along the edge of this cirque is the home of colossal bristlecone pines. Standing as they have for millennia, in their fields of stone, they overlook the desert far below.

When this student and his associate came upon the bristlecones at the timberline, they began to take core samples from several trees, discovering one to be over four thousand years old. Needless to say they were excited, and at some point, their only coring tool broke. The end of the field season was nearing. They asked for, and were granted permission, by the US Forest Service, to cut the tree down.

They had just cut down one of the oldest living organisms on the planet. An earlier group of researchers at Wheeler Peak had given names to these ancient creatures whose growing lives reach back to the third century before Christ. They had named some of these trees. Ancient names like Socrates and Buddha. And then there was Prometheus, named after the god in Greek mythology who was punished for stealing fire from the gods and giving it to humankind. Zeus has Prometheus chained to a rock for an eternity of perpetual torment.[3]

It was the tree named after Prometheus that the geology students had killed. They had cut down a tree that was 4,844 years old.

What happened that day on Wheeler Peak is now viewed as a kind of martyrdom by some bristlecone pine researchers. The inexplicable horror of Prometheus's death served to save the other bristlecone pines from extinction at human hands. You might even say it is to the bristlecone pines what the cross of Jesus is to the human species, a death that brings life to the rest of us. "The royal consciousness leads people to numbness," writes Walter Brueggemann, "especially to numbness about death. It is the task of prophetic . . . imagination to bring people to engage their experiences of suffering to death."[4]

The death of a 4,844-year-old tree and the death of Christ are two sides of a single coin. The death of Prometheus at the tree line on Wheeler Peak is the death of nature at human hands. The death

3. Cohen, *A Garden of Bristlecones*.

4. Brueggemann, *The Prophetic Imagination*, 41.

of Jesus on the Hill of Skulls is the death of humankind, and in both cases, a new human awareness, a new humanity, is awakened.

In the death of that old bristlecone pine the other researchers came to a new appreciation of nature itself. Not only its magnificence, not only our dependence upon nature, but our oneness with nature. *Homo sapiens* do not stand above nature; we stand *within* it.

Remember, good people. Do not forget. God loves "prophetic madmen and women" who challenge the madness. Remember Prometheus. Remember the Hill of Skulls. Do not forget.

We are not above nature. We *are* nature; nature is us.

Bibliography

AB Bookman's Weekly: For the Specialist Book World 76 (1985): 19–27.

Alice in Wonderland, DVD, directed by Tim Burton. Burbank, CA: Walt Disney Pictures, 2010.

Amnesty International. "I Am Troy Davis: The Fight for Abolition Continues." http://www.amnestyusa.org/our-work/cases/usa-troy-davis.

Anderson, Nick. "For Many at Liberty University, Guns and God Go Hand in Hand." *Washington Post*, December 14, 2015. https://www.washingtonpost.com/local/education/for-many-at-liberty-university-guns-and-god-go-hand-in-hand/2015/12/14/3251bfb2-9fc9-11e5-a3c5-c77f2cc5a43c_story.html.

Aquinas, Thomas. *Summa Theologica I–II*. London: Blackfriars, 1969.

Arnold, Matthew. *Empedocles on Etna, and Other Poems*. London: B. Fellowes, 1852.

Baldwin, James. *Notes of a Native Son*. Boston: Beacon, 1955.

Becker, Ernest. *The Denial of Death*. New York: Free Press, 1973.

Berry, Wendell. *The Art of the Commonplace: The Agrarian Essays of Wendell Berry*. Edited by Norman Wirzba. Washington, DC: Counterpoint, 2002.

———. *Jayber Crow: A Novel*. Washington, DC: Counterpoint, 2000.

———. *A Place in Time: Twenty Stories of the Port William Membership*. Berkeley: Counterpoint, 2012.

Boulton, Matthew Myer. *God Against Religion: Rethinking Christian Theology through Worship*. Grand Rapids: Eerdmans, 2008.

Brueggemann, Walter. *The Prophetic Imagination*. 2nd ed. Minneapolis: Augsburg Fortress, 2001.

Camus, Albert. *Notebooks*. New York: Knopf, 1963.

Chesapeake Bay Foundation. "A New Day, a New Way for Oyster Restoration." http://www.cbf.org/how-we-save-the-bay/programs-initiatives/maryland/oyster-restoration/oyster-restoration-on-harris-creek.

Cohan, William D. *Money and Power: How Goldman Sachs Came to Rule the World*. New York: Anchor, 2011.

Cohen, Michael P. *A Garden of Bristlecones: Tales of Change in the Great Basin*. Reno: University of Nevada Press, 1998.

Colby, Frank Moore. *The Colby Essays*. Vol. 2, *Tailor Blood and Other Notes and Comments*. Edited by Clarence Day Jr. New York: Harper and Brothers, 1926.

Cone, James H. *God of the Oppressed*. New York: Seabury, 1975.

Debs, Eugene. "Statement to the Federal Court of Cleveland, Ohio." September 18, 1918. http://rhetoricalgoddess.wikia.com/wiki/Eugene_V._Debs,_Statement_to_the_Court.

Deshler, Charles D. *Afternoons with the Poets*. New York: Harper and Brothers, 1879.

Dillard, Annie. *Teaching a Stone to Talk*. New York: Harper and Row, 1982.

Duchschere, Kevin. "Return of Blackhawk Copters Surprises and Alarms Residents." *Star Tribune*, August 20, 2014. http://www.startribune.com/aug-20-2014-return-of-copters-to-twin-cities-surprises-alarms-residents/271940081/.

Egan, Timothy. "Deconstructing a Demagogue." *New York Times*, January 26, 2012. http://opinionator.blogs.nytimes.com/2012/01/26/deconstructing-a-demagogue/?_r=0.

Fosdick, Harry Emerson. *Dear Mr. Brown: Letters to a Person Perplexed About Religion*. New York: Harper and Brothers, 1961.

Fosdick, Harry Emerson. "Shall the Fundamentalists Win?" *Christian Work* 102 (June 10, 1922) 716–22.

French, Rose. "Minn. Muslims Denounce Attack." *Star Tribune*, September 13, 2012. http://www.startribune.com/minn-muslims-denounce-attacks/169565636/.

Gup, Ted. "Woman of the Woods." *Washington Post*, July 1, 1996. https://www.washingtonpost.com/archive/lifestyle/1996/07/01/woman-of-the-woods/56b76c91-56ee-46af-89ed-de6902e9dc97/.

Gustafson, James M. *Ethics from a Theocentric Perspective*. Vol. 1, *Theology and Ethics*. Chicago: University of Chicago Press, 1981.

Hamilton, Walter, and Nathaniel Popper. "Goldman Sachs Executive's Parting Shots Shock Wall Street." *Los Angeles Times*, March 14, 2012. http://articles.latimes.com/2012/mar/14/business/la-fi-goldman-20120315.

Hazlitt, William. *The Round Table*. New York: Scribner, Welford, 1869.

Irving, John. *The Hotel New Hampshire*. New York: Random House, 1981.

Jefferson, Thomas. *The Papers of Thomas Jefferson*. Edited by Julian P. Boyd et al. Princeton: Princeton University Press, 1950–.

Jones, Deborah. "Animals in the World of St. Basil the Great." Catholic Concerns for Animals, *The Ark* 211 (Spring 2009), accessed August 26, 2016.

Kaufman, Leslie, and Clifford Krauss. "BP Prepares to Take New Tack on Leak after 'Top Kill' Fails." *New York Times*, May 29, 2010. http://www.nytimes.com/2010/05/30/us/30spill.html.

Kierkegaard, Soren. *The Concept of Irony: With Continual Reference to Socrates."* Edited and translated by Howard V. Hong and Edna H. Hong. Princeton: Princeton University Press, 1992.

King, Martin Luther, Jr. "Letter from Birmingham Jail," April 16, 1963.

———. *Strength to Love*. London: Collins, 1977.

Koyoma, Kosuke. *Mount Fuji and Mount Sinai: A Critique of Idols*. Maryknoll, NY: Orbis, 1984.

———. *No Handle on the Cross: An Asian Meditation on the Crucified Mind*. Reprint, Eugene, OR: Wipf & Stock, 2011.

———. *Three Mile an Hour God: Biblical Reflections*. Maryknoll, NY: Orbis, 1979.

———. *Water Buffalo Theology*. 25th anniversary ed. Maryknoll, NY: Orbis, 1999.

Longfellow, Henry Wadsworth. *Courtship of Miles Standish*. Boston: Houghton, Mifflin, 1858.

Manar, Al, ed. *Abdelwahab Meddeb: Le Proche et Le Lointain*. Paris: Broché, 2016.

Margulies, Joseph. *Guantánamo and the Abuse of Presidential Power*. New York: Simon & Schuster, 2006.

———. *What Changed When Everything Changed: 9/11 and the Making of National Identity*. New Haven: Yale University Press, 2013.

Miller, Robert Moats. *Harry Emerson Fosdick: Preacher, Pastor, Prophet*. New York: Oxford University Press, 1985.

Moore, Sebastian. *The Crucified Jesus Is No Stranger*. New York: Paulist, 1959.

———. *The Inner Loneliness*. New York: Crossroad, 1982.

———. *Remembered Bliss: A Book of Spiritual Sonnets*. Edited by Kate Sotejeff-Wilson. Belfast: Lapwing, 2014.

Mora, Camilo, et al. "The Projected Timing of Climate Departure from Recent Variability." *Nature, International Weekly Journal of Science* 502 (2013) 183–87.

Moss, Otis. *Blue Note Preaching in a Post-Soul World: Finding Hope in an Age of Despair*. Louisville: Westminster John Knox, 2015.

Muir, John. *Our National Parks*. Boston: Riverside, 1903.

Otto, Rudolf. *The Idea of the Holy: An Inquiry into the Non-Rational Factor in the Idea of the Divine and its Relation to the Rational*. Translated by John W. Harvey. London: Oxford University Press, 1923.

Parrinder, Geoffrey. *The Routledge Dictionary of Religious & Spiritual Quotations*. London: Routledge, 1990.

Perez, Fabio Y. "Survival Tactics of Indigenous People." University of Wisconsin-Eau Claire, Spring 2005, accessed August 26, 2016. http://academic.evergreen.edu/g/grossmaz/LEEPERFY/.

Pew Research Center, U.S. Politics & Policy. "Stark Racial Divisions in Reactions to Ferguson Police Shootings," August 18, 2014. http://www.people-press.org/2014/08/18/stark-racial-divisions-in-reactions-to-ferguson-police-shooting/.

Plaut, W. Gunther. *The Torah: A Modern Commentary*. New York: Union of American Hebrew Congregations, 1981.

Kraybill, Donald B., Steven M. Nolt, and David L. Weaver-Zercher. *Amish Grace: How Forgiveness Transcended Tragedy*. San Francisco: Jossey-Bass, 2007.

Senate Permanent Subcommittee on Investigations, Hearings. "Wall Street and the Financial Crisis: The Role of Investment Banks." April 27, 2010. http://www.hsgac.senate.gov/subcommittees/investigations/hearings/-wall-street-and-the-financial-crisis-the-role-of-investment-banks.

Shoemaker, Steve. "A Song for Each Kind of Day," *Views from the Edge* (blog), April 12, 2012.

———. "The Man Who Loved Graves." *Views from the Edge* (blog), April 24, 2012. https://gordoncstewart.com/2016/10/15/steve-shoemaker-last-verse/.

———. "Our Family Bush." *Views from the Edge* (blog), July 26, 2014. https://gordoncstewart.com/2014/07/26/our-family-bush/.

———. "What We Are Supposed to Hate." *Views from the Edge* (blog), May 2, 2015. https://gordoncstewart.com/2015/05/02/verse-what-we-are-supposed-to-hate/.

Shriver, Peggy Ann Leu. *The Dancers of Riverside Park and Other Poems*. Louisville: Westminster John Knox, 2001.

Sigourney, L. H. *Poems for the Sea*. Hartford: H. S. Parsons, 1850.

Smith, Greg. "Why I Am leaving Goldman Sachs." *New York Times*, March 14, 2012. http://www.nytimes.com/2012/03/14/opinion/why-i-am-leaving-goldman-sachs.html.

Smithsonian National Museum of Natural History. "The Gulf Oil Spill." Smithsonian Ocean Portal, accessed August 26, 2016. http://ocean.si.edu/gulf-oil-spill.

Stangneth, Bettina. *Eichmann Before Jerusalem: The Unexamined Life of a Mass Murderer*. Translated by Ruth Martin. New York: Knopf, 2014.

Stringfellow, William. *An Ethic for Christians and Other Aliens in a Strange Land*. Reprint, Eugene, OR: Wipf & Stock, 2004.

———. *Imposters of God: Inquiries into Favorite Idols*. Reprint, Eugene, OR: Wipf & Stock, 2006.

———. *A Keeper of the Word: Selected Writings of William Stringfellow*. Edited by Bill Wylie-Kellerman. Grand Rapids: Eerdmans, 1996.

———. *My People Is the Enemy*. New York: Holt, Rinehart and Winston, 1964.

Thoreau, Henry David. "Life Without Principle." *The Atlantic Monthly* 12 (1863): 484–95.

Tillich, Paul. *Systematic Theology*. Vol. 1, *Reason and Revelation; Being and God*. Chicago: University of Chicago Press, 1951.

Toynbee, Arnold J. "Why and How I Work." *Saturday Review*, April 5, 1969.

Turner, Charles Tennyson. *Collected Sonnets: Old and New*. London: C. Kegan Paul & Co., 1880.

West, Cornel. *Race Matters*. New York: Vintage, 1994.

White, Jerry. "Texas Executes 62-Year-Old Great Grandmother Betty Lou Beets." *World Socialist Web Site*. Published by the International Committee of the Fourth International (ICFI), February 26, 2000. http://www.wsws.org/en/articles/2000/02/exec-f26.html.

Wiesel, Elie. *Four Hasidic Masters and Their Struggle against Melancholy.* Notre Dame: University of Notre Dame Press, 1987.

———. *Souls on Fire: Portraits and Legends of Hasidic Masters.* New York: Random House, 1972.

Wilgoren, Jodi. "Citing Issue of Fairness, Governor Clears Out Death Row in Illinois." *New York Times,* January 12, 2003. http://www.nytimes.com/2003/01/12/us/citing-issue-of-fairness-governor-clears-out-death-row-in-illinois.html.

Will, George F. "A Murderer's Warped Idealism." *Washington Post,* November 14, 2014. https://www.washingtonpost.com/opinions/george-f-will-bettina-stangneth-reveals-adolf-eichmanns-warped-idealism/2014/11/14/33de5bba-6b81-11e4-a31c-77759fc1eacc_story.html?utm_term=.680d347bde05.

Withnall, Adam. "Typhoon Haiyan Overshadows UN Climate Change Talks in Poland." *Independent,* November 12, 2013. http://www.independent.co.uk/news/world/asia/typhoon-haiyan-overshadows-un-climate-change-talks-in-poland-8934115.html.

Zuurdeeg, Willem Frederik. *An Analytical Philosophy of Religion.* New York: Abingdon, 1958.

———. *Man Before Chaos: Philosophy Is Born in a Cry.* Prepared for publication by Esther Cornelius Swenson. Nashville: Abingdon, 1968.

Index

Index

Index

Index

Index

Index

Index